Shame on ME—
No more!

God's Double Blessings in Exchange for my Shame"

By

Granotta Farquharson

First Printing, 2023

ISBN: 979-8-88992-054-0

Printed in the United States of America

Publisher: Published by Purpose Publishing House
PurposePublishingHouse@gmail.com
www.PurposePublishingHouse.com

Table of Contents

Foreword

S hame is an emotional experience that every human being encounters at some point in their life. It is a powerful feeling that can impact an individual's psyche, self-worth, and relationships. Shame can mute our authentic self-expression and can leave us feeling isolated and misunderstood.

In this book, Shame on Me – No more: God's Double Blessings in Exchange for my Shame, written by my wife, who has experienced shame, we are given a unique and personal insight into the complexities of this emotion. By sharing her experiences in a vulnerable and honest way, Granotta invites us to explore our relationship with shame and offers us valuable tools to help us navigate this complex emotional territory.

Her willingness to open herself up to vulnerability is a rare gift we should honor and cherish. Through our story, she shows us how it feels to carry shame in a relationship and how it can impact our interactions with our partners.

This book is a must-read for anyone who has experienced shame or wants to understand how shame can impact someone. It is a thoughtful and inspiring work that offers a new perspective on this powerful emotion.

As you read, I invite you to open yourself up to vulnerability as Granotta has done and to explore your relationship with shame with a willingness to learn and grow.

Dr. Jerome Farquharson, DMin

Foreword

I have known Granotta for far too many years to express. She has always been the epitome of style, grace, beauty, and brains. Granotta embodied the myth of a strong black woman whose personal and profession life blossomed beautifully for all to see and admire. Who would have thought that behind the beauty, ashes were smoldering and trying to consume the very air that she breathed?

In this book, "Shame on Me – No More: God's Double Blessings in Exchange for my Shame," Granotta transparently shares the dismal situations from her past that were laid buried in the depths of her soul. No matter how bleak her situation became, God was still able to reveal spiritual secrets that opened the door of prosperity for her.

Over a year ago, four women gathered together virtually, determined to write a memoir to help others. We cried, we laughed, and we supported each other. The origins of our conversations and collaboration helped to give birth to this novel. This memoir used the past mingled with the present to demonstrate God's purpose and plan for your life.

Today, as I write this foreword to her captivating and inspiring memoir, I smile because I'm reminded of our weekly chats and conversations that you will now experience as you read her memoir. Use this book as a template for your growth mindset, and let God continue the work in you.

Reading her book, you will learn how to respond righteously to your challenges and tragedies. When you are faithful to God, He will restore and double the prosperity of your mind, body, and spirit. Trust His plan.

> *Being confident of this very thing, that he which hath begun a good work in you will perform it until the day of Jesus Christ.*
> *- Philippians 1:6*

Dr. Vanessa Howard

Acknowledgments

First and foremost, I thank God for allowing me the opportunity to write and share my story. He brought me through many storms, all for his glory and I am grateful to God to share it with you. Second, I thank my husband Jerome, for loving me unconditionally and not permitting my past to hinder what God had in store for us, I love you! To my two sons, Isaiah and Quentin, who I love to life, what a blessing it is to be your mom. To Mom and Dad, whom I love dearly, thanks for raising me in church and teaching me what the love of God really means. Without my relationship in God I don't know where I would be. To my friend Dr. Vanessa Howard, thanks for one day telling me, "You have a story and you should write about it." Thanks for getting me started on this journey. To some of my besties, Teresa High, and Nafeesah Lester, my sister Gretchen Layton and my aunt Cindy Casey, your encouragement through this process has been extraordinary. I love and appreciate you all for sticking with me. To my friend Stacy Harbor, you sowed the first financial seed into this project, and I am so grateful. I can't thank each of you enough.

Introduction

Do dreams really come true? It's no surprise that at an early age, most of us think we know what we want to be when we grow up. For some, it is a doctor, lawyer, school teacher, or even the President. By the time we reach the age to really make that decision, we've possibly changed our minds several times. As a young girl, my dream was to finish high school, of course, graduate from college, find my dream job, whatever that might be, or get married to someone that would take good care of me, have two children, and then become a stay at home mom and enjoy life. Did it seem possible? ABSOLUTELY. Did it happen? Well, not quite.

We can never predict which road life will take us to reach our dream. For me, I finished high school, started college but didn't finish until well into my adult years, worked at an insurance company, by no means my dream job, got married, did not have kids as planned, and the rest, you'll have to read on to find out. One thing I can say, God had a plan for me, and no matter what my plan was as that little girl, I have found in my adult life that His plan is perfect. The road wasn't easy, but the reward made it worth it.

SHAME ON ME—NO MORE is my story of how God took me through the most difficult times of my life, things I never imagined I would experience, and brought me through victoriously. For years I lost my identity, who God created me to be, hiding behind the many masks of **SHAME**. My intent for this book, first and foremost, is that God will get the glory out of my story; even though it has taken me years to write still, His timing is perfect. Second, my prayer is that if you are experiencing something in your life that has allowed **SHAME** to misrepresent who you are in Christ, steal your identity, or make you feel there is no hope that you will understand what God did for me, just trust the process. He will deliver you.

At the end of each chapter is a section called Lesson Learned. These are short excerpts of me looking back in hindsight on my life and realizing now the lesson I've learned. The lesson was always there. I was blinded to what it was trying to teach me at the time. My prayer is that each lesson will also encourage you, the reader, to apply what I've learned to your situation and be inspired by each scripture reference.

CHAPTER 1

The Message in the Fireplace

To appoint unto them that mourn in Zion, to give unto them beauty for ashes, the oil of joy for mourning, the garment of praise for the spirit of heaviness; that they might be called trees of righteousness, the planting of the LORD, that he might be glorified. - Isaiah 61:2

It was a sweltering hot day. I was glad to be sitting in the living room relaxing with my grandmother, my mom's mother, who I also called "Mama." A cool breeze came from the window unit air conditioner that took up most of the oversized picture window in the front room. The television was blasting because my grandfather was a little hard of hearing. At this time in my life, I had graduated high school, was taking some college courses, worked for the unemployment office downtown, and lived with my grandparents. You see, for most of my childhood, we lived near my grandparents. They both played an intricate part in raising us. As for me, my grandmother was the best grandmother on planet Earth. Having two "mamas" made me feel like the luckiest girl in the world, and being the first granddaughter definitely had its perks.

We lived in a four-family flat on a quiet street around the corner from the neighborhood police station. My grandfather, affectionately known as Pops, owned the flat. It seemed like one of the biggest houses on the street. It was surrounded by tall well-manicured bushes with a large concrete staircase that led to the long porch lined with four glass and wooden doors. On the porch were light gray metal chairs where many conversations of family and friends took place for hours.

Pops and Mama lived in two of the units. They cut a doorway for upstairs access. The other two units were always rented out to family and later friends. At one time, we lived in the upstairs unit and then later moved into the downstairs unit. I really don't know why because the units were pretty much the same. At that time, they were called shotgun houses, meaning you could stand at the front door and shoot a shotgun straight to the backdoor. The layout was a large living room that led directly into a midsize bedroom, a bathroom, a kitchen, and another small room off the kitchen with a basement shared by each of the two units. Because my grandparents lived in two units, they were able to put a dining room in their downstairs room off the living room. The place where many Thanksgiving and Christmas dinners were held for the entire family. In our unit, our parents slept in one of the bedrooms, and my brother and I shared the other. I spent most of my time in the humungous backyard equipped with mulberry and peach trees.

My parents worked, so my older brother, of 13 months, and I spent our summers being watched by our grandmother. We played outside with all the neighborhood kids from sun-up until sundown. We could play all day, only breaking for a fried bologna or tuna fish sandwich and a tall glass of flavored Kool-Aid. We knew we had to be home by the time the street lights came on, our built-in alarm clock. During school days, we were either walked to school by our mom or grandmother until we were old enough to walk alone with our friends. I attended the neighborhood elementary school, which was about five city blocks from our house, from kindergarten to 5th grade. I liked school and tried to do my best to make good grades.

I didn't have many friends growing up. I had three friends in the neighborhood with my best friend who lived next door. We would spend many hours at each other's house, either playing with paper dolls, making doll clothes for our Barbies, or dancing and listening to music. I was somewhat naïve and trusted everyone until I found out later, "You can't trust everyone." Not understanding the importance of being yourself as a child, I resorted to being a people pleaser. Always trying to "make" people like me, wondering if I was good enough. This practice carried on from my adolescent life to well into my adult years.

Before starting sixth grade, my parents decided to move our family to our own house where for the first time, I would have my own room. Sharing a room with now three brothers was getting pretty old. I had mixed emotions. Thoughts of excitement warred with feelings of devastation. Was getting my pretty yellow bedroom worth being far away from my friends, my school, and most of all, my grandparents? I never said a word about how I felt. I suppressed those feelings as I often did, like sweeping trash under a kitchen rug, never to be seen by anyone. After moving, we visited my grandparents often. Every time we piled into my dad's 1965 burgundy Pontiac Catalina and headed in that direction, it brought feelings of exhilaration that one could see by the sparkle in my eyes and the dancing in my feet. That only lasted about a year. By the time I finished 6th grade, my dad's job had transferred him to Houston, Texas. Another move, this time far more disturbing than the first move. No family, no friends, no church, no playdates, and most of all, no grandparents. Not my mom's or my dad's parents, NO GRANDPARENTS in Texas. I was not happy, but I never verbally expressed it.

Texas brought many new adventures into our everyday lives. We lived in a neighborhood where most of our neighbors spoke English and Spanish, but mostly Spanish. We started a new school, a new church, new friends, and a new baby. Yes, finally, I was not the only girl. Even though twelve years apart, I was so thankful to wear the crown of "Big Sister." Our stay in Texas didn't last very long. Circumstances with my dad's job landed us right back in St. Louis during the summertime two years later.

I was about to enter high school when we returned to St. Louis. Decisions had to be made quickly before school started. Even though it was not the ideal plan, our family was divided for the sake of space. My parents and my three younger siblings lived with my dad's parents, and my older brother and I lived, guess where, with my mom's parents, my beloved grandparents. I had gravely missed them and was totally beside myself at the new temporary living arrangements.

My grandfather always worked several jobs taking care of his family and continued even after his children were grown and moved out. My grandmother stayed home most of her life, enjoying church, taking care of the home, and cooking scrumptious meals daily. Most of my time was consumed with doing school work, helping around the house, attending church, and spending lots of time with just myself. Even though my parents eventually moved, I remained at the same high school and sometimes lived with my parents and sometimes with my grandparents. After graduating high school, starting college, and working, I moved in permanently with my grandparents because it was easier for me to get back and forth to work from their house than from where my parents lived.

I spent many evenings laughing and talking with my grandmother over the sound of the television, sharing with each other our daily events. My grandmother was short in stature and yet a giant in the eyes of God. She accepted Christ as her Lord and Savior at the tender age of 12 and loved talking about God's goodness and sharing stories from the Bible. She was a faithful member of her church, which was within walking distance of our home. We often walked to a weekly daytime prayer meeting or Bible study in the summertime. She would rest in her rocking chair for hours, reading her good book. She always had a word of encouragement or a question that would provoke me to get my Bible to search for answers. This was always a challenge for me because I felt that as much time as she spent in her Bible, she knew all the answers. How could I even measure up to her?

One evening as my grandfather napped on the couch, I heard my grandmother say, "I need you to turn down the tv; I have something to talk to you about." I got up from my chair, walked over to the large floor-model television, and lowered the volume. With her soft-spoken voice and an expression on her face that somewhat startled me, she glared into the imitation fireplace under the mantle and quietly murmured, "I see you in the ashes." Confused and not sure I heard her correctly, I asked, "What did you say?" She pointed to the fireplace and repeated in the same soft tone, "I see you in the ashes." Thoughts began to race through my head. Did she think I was going to be in a fire? Was I going to do something to burn the house down? What did she mean? She never explained her statement. She just spoke, "But you'll be all right." I asked why she said that, but she put a smile on her face and said God told me to tell you "you'll be all right." From that day forward, she never uttered another word about the incident; for her, everything was normal. However, I couldn't let it go and thought, what on earth am I to do with this information?

For days, the statement, "I see you in the ashes," lingered in every possible corner of my mind. Ashes, ashes, why ashes? I didn't share what she told me with anyone else. Not my parents, my brother, or any of my friends. As usual, I obsessed internally, allowing these thoughts to replay constantly. I had to find out what she was trying to tell me. Being the introvert that I am, resorting to my upstairs bedroom and mentally processing it like I did most things was natural. However, my bedroom was next to my grandparents, so privacy was out of the question. Paranoia set in, and negative thought patterns about fires and ashes caused restless nights and mental fatigue. I went on a mission to get to the bottom of this.

I was a choir director at my church and worked faithfully with the music ministry. I remembered that one of the older gentlemen who worked with us had often shared the dreams and visions he frequently encountered. Just from his conversations, I knew he had the gift of interpretation. Still hesitant to share with anyone, I chose not to call him but decided to wait to see him at church. Working my nerves to approach him the next time I went to church was as difficult as a student confessing to the teacher of cheating on the final exam. He wasn't there that day. My thought was that maybe this was a sign that I was not supposed to share this with anyone. Maybe this is for me to figure out on my own. No way, I felt I needed to get to him as soon as possible. The next time I went to church was on a Wednesday evening for Bible study. I got there early and looked frantically for him to get an answer to this mystery. Finally, I saw him and swiftly made my way over to him. I told him I had an encounter with my grandmother that left me quite puzzled. I explained what happened and what she shared with me. He almost had the same shocked look as I did when she first voiced the words to me. Without hesitation, he stated, "Well, in the Bible, ashes symbolize grief or mourning. Let's talk after Bible study." When the service ended, I waited until practically everyone in the sanctuary had cleared out. He walked through the door as if he had been looking for me and sat beside me on the long front pew. He began to search his Bible for scriptures and read several to me. When he got to the last scripture, he read it with such excitement in his voice, *"To appoint unto them that mourn in Zion, to give unto them beauty for ashes, the oil of joy for mourning, the garment of praise for the spirit of heaviness; that they might be called trees of righteousness, the planting of the LORD, that he might be glorified."* I was stunned as I sat and listened. I felt a tear welling up in my eye but was hoping that it would not drop as well as a humongous knot in my stomach. I told him, "But this doesn't make sense. I'm not in mourning." I thought, who's going to die? My parents? My grandparents? Any of my relatives? My friends? Who? I could not imagine losing any of them or anyone close to me. He could see the confusion written all over my face. Ironically, he ended our conversation with the same words as Mama did, "You'll be all right." He walked me out with his arm around my shoulder and with a pleasant grin as he restated, "You'll be all right."

In my study time, I began to dissect the scripture, beauty for ashes, oil of joy for mourning, and a garment of praise for the spirit of heaviness. It appeared there was a tradeoff of good for bad. But still, how did this apply to me? Eventually, I buried it in the deep dark basement of my mind. Pondering every time someone got sick if they would be the candidate to usher in my season of mourning. I tried to focus on something positive from that conversation with Mama and the gentleman. What was my takeaway? They both told me I'd be all right, and that's what I was left with. I figured one day I'd understand it, hopefully. It took years before I found out what they both expressed to me. Not at all what I thought it would be.

Years passed, and the memories of that day with my grandmother became a blur. Life seemed great. I didn't finish college but landed a job that allowed me to expand from a receptionist to a marketing representative, and a few years later, I married the guy I had dated since high school. As we prepared to get married, marital counseling wasn't really an option, so many issues and questions that should have been dealt with were never addressed. As any couple coming together as one, we both had closets full of skeletons that we felt were things of the past and thought we'd just leave them in the past. We had a beautiful church wedding surrounded by about 300 members of our family and friends. His family adored me, and my family loved him. We were a typical family where both of us worked outside the home, attended church, and spent most of our free time together, shopping, eating out, and enjoying time with close friends. We both worked in the church singing in the choir and various other areas of ministry. We had been married for almost six years and had rented two different apartments when we finally decided it was time to purchase our first home. We both were so excited. We searched and searched, looking at several homes, trying to find the one that would best suit our needs, desires, and, most of all, our budget. As I saw it, life was going great. So far, so good, or so I thought!

Lesson learned: Confidence

Confidence — The dictionary defines confidence as *a feeling or consciousness of one's powers or of reliance on one's circumstances, faith, or belief that one will act in the right, proper, or effective way.* Even though I didn't quite understand what the future held for me, and neither was I one hundred percent confident that what my grandmother told me would become a reality, I was scared. I realize now that God wanted me to trust Him no matter what. What she shared with me left me baffled. God knew the plan He had for me, and that He was ordering my steps, but for me, I was clueless. He never wanted me to put confidence in what my grandmother told me but to put my confidence in Him—trusting that He would be with me. Hebrews 4:16 tells us, *"Let us then with confidence draw near to the throne of grace, that we may receive mercy and find grace to help in time of need."* This scripture encourages me that even in my frailty, I have continual access to grace and mercy. No matter your situation, stand on God's word and be confident that His plan is perfect for your life. Think of something you could use to boost confidence and ask God to meet you right where you are. He'll do it!

CHAPTER 2

The Shock of My Life

*Many are the afflictions of the righteous, but the LORD delivers him out of them all. - **Psalm 34:19***

The quest continued. We made several offers on different homes, but for one reason or another, our bids were not accepted. Finally, in November of 1992, we were scheduled to close on our very own cozy starter home of two bedrooms and one bath. It had a spacious living room with a dining room off the kitchen and a full basement. When we walked into the house, we knew it was the home for us, AND it was right around the corner from my mom's only sister, my favorite aunt. Unfortunately, we ran into several obstacles trying to secure the purchase. When we got to the closing, we discovered that the owner, who was the neighbor next door, had not secured the gas inspection as promised, and once again, another brick wall hit us dead in the face. The title company extended our closing from Tuesday until Thursday to allow us time to get the inspection completed. I called the gas company as soon as we arrived back at our apartment from the unsuccessful closing, explaining our dilemma.

The lady on the other end of the phone, although very polite, stated, "Ma'am, I understand your situation; however, there is no way we can get anyone to your home by tomorrow. The earliest I can get someone out there would be Saturday morning." As tears streamed down my face, I explained, "Saturday is not acceptable. The inspection has to be done by Thursday's closing date." She reiterated, "There is nothing I can do." We prayed and prayed and believed that God somehow was going to work this out and help us cross this last hurdle to purchasing our first home. My husband wasn't worried, but unfortunately, that wasn't my testimony. I felt as if my entire body was shaking like a leaf barely hanging onto a branch in boisterous high winds. That night I tossed and turned, wondering what would happen the next day. What could I do? Absolutely nothing. I got up the next morning, went to work, and started all over again, making calls to the gas company and asking the woman who answered the phone if I could speak with her supervisor. She forwarded my call to a gentleman, reinforcing what she had already stated. By this time, I had given up. My normal lunch buddies came to my desk, assuming I would be joining them for lunch, and blurted, "Let's go." With disgust written all over my face, I grumbled, "Not today, ladies. I have a lot on my mind." I resorted to grabbing a cold iced tea and driving around in my car alone to try and relieve some of the tension. I returned to work and tried to get some work done to no avail. Right before the end of the day, I received a call from the title company. I just knew they were calling to tell us they were closing our file, and we did not get the house. Instead, the woman on the other end communicated, "The owner informed us that the gas company had been at your new home on Wednesday morning to do the inspection, and everything was set for you all to close on Thursday." My body was as limp as a wet rag full of water and suds. I called my husband with the good news, and we rejoiced that somehow the Lord had made way for us. We closed on Thursday and moved that weekend. When we went into the house, there was a pink slip attached to the door from the gas company. It was handwritten, and in the place where the inspector's name was supposed to be, there were numbers. I didn't pay much attention to the numbers; I was just glad that it showed the inspection was successfully completed. Saturday, as I was working in the kitchen unpacking boxes, the beige wall telephone rang, and the gentlemen on the other end said, "Good morning, Mrs. I am calling from Laclede Gas to inform you that the inspector will be there shortly to do the inspection as scheduled." I hesitated in uncertainty and explained, "Sir, the inspector came on Wednesday, and we were able to close on Thursday." The next sentence that came out of his mouth sent a shock through my body that had me on a high that I could not explain. He said, "Ma'am, that's impossible because I run the department that schedules all inspections, and we never scheduled one for your home on Wednesday." He asked whose name was on the card. I responded there wasn't a name, just numbers. I read the numbers back to him, and he said, "I'm not familiar with that ID number, so as stated, my inspector will be there shortly." All I could do was hang up the phone and begin to praise the Lord for our gas inspection angel! Sent by non-other than Jesus Christ himself. I couldn't wait for my husband to get home to share with him what I had just encountered. We both praised God together for the miracle He performed before our very own eyes. We spent the next couple of weeks simply enjoying being homeowners.

That same month being so enthusiastic about our first home purchase, we wanted to share our excitement with everyone, so we planned a housewarming. Everything was going great. We worked diligently decorating our home with a mixture of new and used furniture pieces and decorative artwork on the walls to greet our friends and family. We wanted everyone to enjoy an evening of celebrating our new humble abode. Regrettably, all did not go as planned. The wonderful evening turned into an awful nightmare. While preparing hot and cold finger foods for the evening, suddenly, my husband began to feel ill. Pain struck his body, and he spent most of the afternoon in the bathroom throwing up and later developed a fever. About an hour before the guest was due to arrive, my husband insisted that I stay and enjoy the evening while a close friend took him to the hospital. Not happy with the decision, I stayed for the evening festivities. As the guest began to arrive, they were shocked that I was home alone. Many tried to cheer me up but realized it was hopeless. My mind was on what was going on at the hospital. Needless to say, the housewarming ended early, and later that evening, my husband was sent home with a diagnosis of food poisoning. After about a week of watching what he ate, he returned to his normal routine. Life was going great, or so I thought!

We enjoyed celebrating Christmas and New Year's Eve in our new home. Month after month, we focused on getting our house just as we wanted it. We were extremely busy. We both worked full-time jobs, attended Bible study, choir rehearsals, all-day Sunday services, and worked on various church committees. Our annual church convention was scheduled for June; we both worked on the planning committee of it. Weekly deadlines were mandated, but everyone involved worked hard and anticipated the excitement of this event. The week before the conference, unexpectantly, my husband got sick again and landed back in the hospital. At this point, the repeated visits to the hospital were taking a toll on me. Yes, I was **ASHAMED**. I questioned, "Why is he always sick?" The doctors ran a series of tests once again, searching for a diagnosis. Finally, he was diagnosed with pneumonia and remained in the hospital. He desperately wanted to leave the hospital, and after a week, he was finally discharged. The stipulation of his being allowed to go home was that he was prescribed antibodies to be administered intravenously by a registered nurse. She was scheduled to come to the house the day he was discharged to set up the IV and repeat her visit daily for a week. It had been an extremely difficult week of working, trips back and forth to the hospital, and keeping things running at home.

After we got home and situated, there was a knock on the door to let me know the nurse had arrived. Exhaustion had overtaken me, but I politely opened the door and announced, "We've been expecting you; please come in." I escorted her to the dining room table where my husband was sitting waiting for her. I went and laid across the bed in our bedroom right down the hallway on the right. I could hear the nurse talking to him and going over the paperwork. She asked him to confirm his date of birth, address, marital status, and a host of other questions. Then she got to the medical questions. She asked,

"You were diagnosed in the hospital with pneumonia." I heard him respond yes. Then I heard her say, "And you have full-blown AIDS!" I listened attentively but nervously for his response and heard dead silence. Evidently, he nodded his head with an affirmative YES because I heard her reply, "Oh, I'm so sorry." I can't even describe the array of emotions that went through my mind and body. Anger, rage, hurt, betrayal, embarrassment, and most of all, **SHAME**, to name a few. I immediately closed the bedroom door because I didn't want to hear another word of the conversation going on in my dining room. I laid there in a sea of tears, feeling sick to my stomach. I just knew my breakfast, lunch, and whatever else I had consumed that day were about to be splattered all over my bedroom floor. Past rumors that I had heard were now a reality. I made a choice to trust someone who assured me that those very rumors were a thing of his past. How in the world was I going to move on from this one? I had no idea what kind of life was ahead for me, if it would be a life at all. Left in total disarray, I vaguely heard the front door open. I knew then that the nurse had completed what she had come to do. She uttered, "I'll see you tomorrow." The thoughts rushed through my head, "Tomorrow… I never want to see you again." This woman has just shattered my whole world. Then it hit me. Wait a minute; I couldn't blame her.

I didn't know exactly where my husband was in the house, so I chose not to come out of the bedroom. In all honesty, I really wanted to climb out the bedroom window and run away. I lingered in the room for a few minutes because I didn't want to talk to him, see him or hear anything he had to say. All I wanted to do was get out of the house. Thoughts were all over the place. Where could I go? Who could I call? Should I tell anyone? Because of the dreadful **SHAME**, I convinced myself to keep silent. Don't call my parents, my siblings, my friends, my pastor, no one. I decided that night I would handle this on my own. Big mistake! I remembered that there was a dinner that night for all the workers that helped put the conference together. Even though I was physically, mentally, and emotionally distraught, I decided to go there. I didn't even change clothes. I opened the bedroom door and walked across the hall to the bathroom to dry my eyes, blow my nose, wash my face, and throw a splash of cologne on me. I came out, gathered my purse and keys, raced out the garage door, got in my car, and left.

I drove the longest route to the restaurant with tears streaming down my face. I needed time to process what I had just heard. I began to cry out to the Lord, no fancy prayer, simply "Lord, Help Me." I second-guessed myself thinking, "Is this a good idea? Surely someone will notice that I'm a total basket case." I rolled down the windows to let the fresh air dry my eyes and hopefully remove the redness. When I arrived, I put a smile on my face and the first of many masks I wore throughout this journey. As difficult as it was, I pulled into the parking lot of the restaurant and examined myself in the overhead mirror. Thankfully my eyes weren't as red and puffy; however, I felt like the word **SHAME** was plastered across my forehead. I entered the restaurant and was ushered to the banquet room, where large long tables were assembled. It appeared that I was entering a room full of people that were missioned to judge me that evening.

Practically everyone knew that he had been sick and was in the hospital. The question for the evening was, "How's your husband?" My repeated response which I had rehearsed in the car, was, "He's home and doing better." Most of the evening was a blur. I fixed a plate and grabbed a seat as quickly as possible to avoid any interaction with more people. As the evening went on, we ate dinner, which I continuously rearranged on my plate, trying to act as if I was enjoying it. I lingered around with some of the last people to leave the restaurant. I figured I would stay out as late as possible to give my husband time to go to bed. Once headed back, I repeated my drive there and took the longest route back home. My scheme for the evening worked; when I got home, he had gone to bed. I knew I had to go to work the next day, so I prepared for that and went to bed in the second bedroom. I fought sleep the entire night, but as daybreak drew near, I got up, showered, got dressed, and left. When I arrived at work, I did my usual, accompanied my co-workers to the cafeteria for my normal warmed blueberry muffin and chilled orange juice, and resorted back to my cubical to try to focus on my task for the day. I found myself staring at walls most of the day, reliving the conversation between my husband and the nurse, and not getting a lot accomplished. As the closing time arrived, I gathered my belongings and prepared to leave. I had taken off the remainder of the week to attend the convention, so I was grateful I didn't have to come back to the office and pretend that everything was okay in front of my coworkers.

By the time I got home that evening, the nurse had been there to administer the antibiotics. The words of conversation between my husband and me were few and far between. He finally asked me to come into the living room. I took my time and reluctantly entered the room and sat on the loveseat facing him while he sat on the couch. He first affirmed to me, "I love you, and I didn't mean to hurt you." I was completely numb as he continued to talk and explain. I was at a total loss for words and remained silent. Any words that I wanted to share seemed to be stuck in my head, and I couldn't formulate them to release from my lips. He never gave a satisfying explanation, and at that point, I wasn't sure if I was open to hearing it. I felt there wasn't any clarification that would help me feel any better. Originally, I had planned to stay home with him that week; however, things had drastically changed, and all I wanted was to get out of the house. I decided I would attend as much of the convention as I could. That evening, I scoped the house to make sure everything was in order. He had eaten dinner, the dishes were washed and put away, and he was feeling okay, so I left for church. As the week went on, I made sure he was okay and had something to eat before I left. On Friday night, it seemed the service was orchestrated just for me. The guest choir sang, *"He's working it out for you,"* and the preacher preached from Psalm 34:19, *"Many are the afflictions of the righteous, but the LORD delivers him out of them all."* His sermon topic was "God delivers us from them ALL!" He emphasized "ALL," reminding us that God did not pick and choose which afflictions to deliver us from but that He delivers us from all of them. That night was such a comfort for me. I felt that God was speaking directly to me. As the days passed, my husband fully recovered from pneumonia and returned to work. I still had many decisions to make. We remained together, but it always seemed that there was an elephant in the room. Our lives had taken a major shift from what I thought was the best life to a life of total uncertainty. It just wasn't the same.

All while this was going on, we also found out my aunt (my mom's only sister) had been diagnosed with Breast Cancer. Living so close to her, I spent many days caring for her. Walking through that experience with her was so difficult. Then adding what I had just learned about my husband was quite overwhelming. The months ahead were filled with many doctors' visits with both my aunt and my husband. Talk about draining every ounce of energy. Most of the time, I felt like a walking zombie. Taking care of myself was put on the back burner while assuming responsibilities for both. As the months flew by, my husband seemed to get better, but my aunt's health was swiftly declining. We were preparing to celebrate Thanksgiving when she took a turn for the worse. The day before Thanksgiving, she passed away.

Lesson learned: Refuge

Refuge, based on dictionary.com, is *shelter or protection from danger, trouble, etc.* Whether it was an angel to step in for the inspection or His presence to meet me in the bedroom as I heard the news of my husband, He was my refuge. Psalm 46:1 states, "*God is our refuge and strength, a very present help in trouble.*" Many times, I didn't feel God and even questioned whether He had abandoned me. Not realizing then that He was always with me. Although I had read the dictionary definition of refuge, my experiences taught me the true meaning.

This verse is a promise, an assurance that our help lies in Him alone. There is no need to doubt when we stand on that promise.

What situation in your life are you dealing with that you feel God has left you? I guarantee you He hasn't. He's right there with you, no matter how dark it seems. Hold on to His promises. The scripture states He is a present help, meaning at the very minute you need Him, He's there.

CHAPTER 3

A Load Lifted

*Come unto me, all ye that labour and are heavy laden, and I will give you rest. - **Matthew 11:28***

Losing my aunt took an unbelievable toll on me. She was more like an older sister to me than an aunt, and I missed her tremendously. Grief had overtaken me, but I tried my best to continue life with a business-as-usual attitude. My load seemed extremely heavy. I spent many nights drenching my pillow in tears, not really figuring out if I was crying over her or my husband. Questions bombarded my head to the point where I kept a steady headache and resorted to popping Tylenol on a regular basis. It was the holiday season, and as much as I loved that time of year, the festivities of Christmas were the last thing on my mind. My husband was doing surprisingly well physically, and as long as he wasn't sick, I could pretty much hide my feelings. No one would know how I fought the **SHAME** of something I didn't do. I continued wearing a mask that everything was all right, and by that time, that mask fit pretty well. After all, nobody knew what was going on, so I thought until I figured out what to do next, nobody would know. In front of everyone, we looked like a happily married couple.

The first week in December, we were invited out of town to a wedding. I thought this would be a great getaway and an opportunity to share some joy with others and get my mind off all the events of the past couple of months. We packed and traveled the six-hour drive to the wedding. As we entered the sanctuary adorned with beautiful flowers, lit candles, and soft music in the background, our hearts were enlightened by the much-needed change of scenery. We enjoyed celebrating with our dear friends. As we were preparing to travel back, my body began to shut down, and that dreaded flu bug attacked me. I felt as if I had been hit with a ton of bricks. I practically slept the entire drive home. I was so out of it I didn't notice he wasn't feeling good either. After we got back home that Sunday evening, we unpacked the car, sat, and tried to eat a light snack before heading to bed. We were both totally exhausted. We individually called in sick on Monday and tried to regain strength for the rest of the week. Apparently, that trip took a major toll on his body. It seemed he never fully recovered from the strain of driving the long distance. I went to work on Tuesday, but he took off another day to get himself together. By Wednesday, he had returned to his job, not feeling his best but able to manage a day's work. We came back to strenuous rehearsals preparing for our New Year's Eve concert and Watch Meeting Service. Some rehearsals he would participate in, and some he was too weak to attend. The night of the concert, he wasn't feeling his greatest but was determined to go anyway. Halfway through the concert, I noticed he was nowhere to be seen. He had landed in the nurse's lounge eating saltine crackers due to what he thought was a very upset stomach. It was a long service which made matters worse. The usual after-midnight breakfast with choir members wasn't even a consideration because of how he felt. He was in so much pain that we went straight home. I wanted to take him to the emergency room, but he insisted on going home, hoping that going to bed and getting some rest would make him feel better.

The wee hours of the morning were literally terrifying. He moaned and groaned, complaining that the pain in his side had become unbearable. Yet he maintained his grounds that he was not going to the hospital on New Year's Day. I called his sister, who was a registered nurse, and she advised me to get him to the hospital as soon as possible. When we arrived, the emergency room was wall-to-wall with people with various injuries and illnesses. The wait was so long, but he was finally taken into an examination room. After running several tests and taking many measures to control the pain, he was admitted to the hospital. I had no idea what to think. Here we were, back in the hospital again, wondering what the outcome of this visit would be. Once he was resting, I managed to get away and go home from being in the hospital for hours. I drove home with impaired vision due to the flood of tears falling from my eyes. My words were short and to the point, "Lord, Help Me!" He remained in the hospital, and each day they ran a different test to determine what was causing the excruciating pain.

The hospital was very generous to us and allowed me to stay overnight whenever I wanted to. It was the weekend, and I decided to stay Friday night because Saturday was his birthday. We always made a big deal of birthdays with dinner, cake, and lots of presents. Unfortunately, he did not feel like celebrating. His sister, his godmother, and I decided to have a makeshift party in his hospital room. Later that same day, the doctors entered his room with very grim, glassy looks and told us their extremely disturbing findings. The female doctor, surrounded by a host of interns, explained to us that he had something called Kaposi Sarcoma (KS). They used a lot of medical terminologies that left me in total confusion about what they were talking about. His sister being a nurse, seemed to understand, and I was assured she would explain it to me later. Then they said something that was all too familiar to me, the big C word. Kaposi Sarcoma (KS) was AIDS-related cancer that had started in his liver. According to the American Cancer Society website, KS *is a cancer that develops from the cells that line lymph or blood vessels. It usually appears as tumors on the skin or on mucosal surfaces such as inside the mouth, but these tumors can also develop in other parts of the body, such as in the lymph nodes (bean-sized collections of immune cells throughout the body), the lungs, or the digestive tract. The abnormal cells of KS form purple, red, or brown blotches or tumors on the skin. These affected areas are called lesions. The skin lesions of KS most often show on the legs or face.* What a birthday present. The doctor continued talking in terms that we didn't quite understand, but we did gather that he needed to start chemotherapy immediately that day, on his birthday. The news was absolutely devastating and another issue that I had to process. I could not formulate a complete sentence. My thoughts were racing like fast-moving vehicles on the track of the Indianapolis 500. How could

I process what I had just heard or even the next turn of events? I watched my aunt and chemotherapy's effects on her body; all I could think was, no, not AGAIN! Feeling as if I couldn't take another bit of bad news, I decided to go home that night alone. I figured the first treatment would not be as harsh on his body as the weeks to come, so I left the hospital. Crying all the way home resulted in another piercing headache. I only could think about taking some Tylenol PM, getting in my bed, lying in a fetal position, and falling asleep. And that's what I did.

I returned to the hospital the following day, feeling as if I hadn't had an ounce of sleep. I parked in the underground parking garage and started what seemed like a two-mile walk to his room. Seeing different expressions on people's faces made me wonder what they were experiencing. Did they just lose a loved one? Did they just get some horrible news? Maybe by chance, someone received great news, like a negative test result. Of course, I pondered, was anyone dealing with what I was faced with? In my mind, the answer was a definite no. No one could possibly be as devasted as I was. As I entered the elevator packed with people, more expressions and more thoughts; I had to get myself together. I didn't want what I was feeling to be plastered all over my face. I put on a happy face and entered his room. He was in a very good mood. He wasn't in any pain, and there were no visual signs of the negative effects of the chemotherapy. We sat quietly, switching from one tv program to another well into the evening hours. Later, I stepped out to grab a salad from the hospital cafeteria to return in time for his dinner tray to be delivered to his room. We talked while eating, and to my surprise, he asked, "So what do you want for your birthday?" Our birthdays were a few days apart, and with everything going on, I hadn't given celebrating my birthday a second thought. I replied, "Don't worry about my birthday; just focus on getting better and getting out of here." As visiting hours drew near, I said my goodbyes and left for the evening. I went home only to repeat the same routine the next day and each evening after work for the remainder of his stay in the hospital. On the day of my birthday, he had his sister buy me an array of lovely gifts. She told me, "Girl, he has worried me about getting these gifts for you." Despite his illness and what he was experiencing, it made me feel great that he didn't want my birthday to pass without being celebrated. Things changed as the weeks went by. The chemo wretched through his body and began to tear it down. Even though many people wanted to visit him, some were concerned, and, of course, some were nosey, we decided on no visitors. The strain that entertaining took on his body was too much for him to handle. He lost his hair, and his weight began to shed. As I looked at him, I became what many may think of as selfish because I wondered what would happen to me. Should I just leave? I felt I couldn't leave because there would be millions of questions about why I left him when he was so sick. I didn't want to do anything that would cause people to talk about us, even though I failed to realize they were already talking. I was still trying to hide the inevitable. I fought these thoughts, but in my heart, I really wanted to see him healed and return to normal.

There was a ray of sunshine through this whole cancer ordeal. I could now tell people he had cancer without mentioning AIDS. I was able to put that into practice when a sister called me with her apologies about my husband. AIDS was not a common word at that time and was hardly ever communicated, especially in the church. However, this particular sister wasn't shy about calling a spade a spade and actually used the word. She said to me, "I heard your husband has AIDS." As **SHAME** gripped my body, I could not believe what I was hearing. My response was, "Oh, my husband has cancer." To my surprise, she persisted, and so did I, "He has cancer." I hung up the phone, grateful when the conversation ended, and began crying like a baby. I questioned, how did she find out? Was my plan a failure? I thought I could just hide it and not have to explain to anyone what was really going on. Who else knew? My stomach felt as if there were millions of knots pulling against each other. This seemed like one of the worst days of my life. Yet I made a choice not to talk to anyone.

I tried my best to focus on other things and not on what was right in front of me. I was writing a play for Easter, and I used that as a catalyst to keep my sanity. My husband encouraged me to write the play and insisted that I work on it as much as my mental stability allowed me. That included weekly rehearsals, which I occasionally was able to attend, and other times delegated the task to others.

Eventually, my daily routine was to go to work and then head to the hospital. Some nights I would spend the night, and on others, I would head home, possibly work on the play and repeat it the next day. My car became my quiet place where I would repeatedly talk to the Lord. I questioned God, was this really the plan that you had for my life? Did I screw up? How will I ever get through this? I asked the infamous question, Why me? I felt none of my questions were being answered, or maybe I ignored the answers because they weren't the answers I wanted to hear.

He was finally discharged from the hospital. That day was bittersweet. He was excited to finally go home, but it was total uncertainty for me. The husband that went into the hospital on the first of January no longer existed. He looked and talked differently; he was very weak and very sick. Because of the KS, lesions formed on his body, with one obvious on his forehead. I had no idea how I was going to manage him, our home, and work all by myself. I had a village that I had not utilized that stepped up to the plate. His sister was a tremendous help to me. His godmother moved in with us and stayed with him while I worked. Nurses came around the clock to administer meds and to give me much-needed breaks. One would come for four hours on Sunday mornings to allow me to attend church. That's where I gained my strength. Even though I never talked about it, my church family supported me. My family offered to be there for me around the clock even though I often neglected their help.

Once he came home, thankfully, we had no return visits to the hospital. One cold brisk evening, the first week of March, my aunt called and asked if she could come by and give me a hand. I did not want to turn any help away, after all, she was family, and I really didn't know how to say no; I resentfully said sure. The only problem was that she was a registered nurse. I knew if she saw him, especially the large lesion on his forehead, she would immediately know the diagnosis. His godmother had left for the evening, so her visit was a perfect opportunity for me to get out of the house. She arrived about an hour later after her call. The knock on the door sent a rush of bottled-up nerves throughout my entire being. She told me, "I want you to get out of the house and go do something for yourself." Unfortunately, I had not been taking care of myself, and I realized that this was not the evening to focus on myself. No self-care for me. I knew I had better get to my parents and finally tell them what I had been dealing with for the past eight months. I thought if I didn't, for sure, my aunt, my dad's sister would. I called my parents to let them know I was on my way. The fifteen-minute drive to their home seemed like an eternity.

The front door was open, and they were patiently waiting for me. I tried my best to keep my composure, but that was a complete failure. As I walked through the door with tears meeting under my chin, it appeared that I was walking into a courtroom to be interrogated. What was I thinking? After all, they were my parents. Why these feelings? Unfortunately, I had chosen to exclude them from this fiasco that I had been dealing with. I raced down the 3-foot hallway that seemed like ten or more feet. I found myself in the oversized living room and immediately made a mad dash for the soft burgundy plush sofa, where I collapsed. To my surprise, I was able to let it all out. I explained, "I just couldn't talk about it to anyone because **SHAME** had a grip on me that I wasn't able to release." They both listened attentively and began to cry along with me. After about an hour of conversation, I felt as if a load had been lifted off me. My parents' first response was, "We knew; we just wanted you to be comfortable coming to us." They embraced me, told me how much they loved me and supported me, and assured me that everything would be ok. The evening ended with prayer, and I headed back home.

While driving home, I thought of the scripture, *"Come unto me, all ye that labour and are heavy laden, and I will give you rest."* Matthew 11:28. I felt so much better; not only had I rested in my parents' arms, but I could feel myself resting in the arms of Jesus. By the time I got back, the house was very quiet. My husband was asleep; I hugged my aunt and told her, "Thank you so much. I didn't exactly do something for myself as you suggested, but what I did do was exactly what I needed, and had you not come, I would have put it off. Good night." I walked her to the door, locked it, and began to retire for the evening. We never talked about what she learned that night or her experience with my husband. As I laid in my bed, as usual, thoughts rushed through my head. Why hadn't I talked to my parents? Why did I wait so long? I realized talking to them would uncover feelings, thoughts, and emotions I didn't want to deal with. I imagined them asking me questions I didn't want to answer or didn't have answers to. Questions like, how did he get AIDS? Didn't I know? Why didn't I leave the day the nurse came to our house with the dreadful diagnosis of AIDS? To admit that I chose to ignore the signs was too much for me to handle. I trusted him when we decided to get married, that everything I had heard about him was of the past, and that he truly loved God and loved me. He and I never talked about how he contracted the disease. So instead of talking to my parents or anyone, I kept it all bundled up inside of me. After all, I felt totally embarrassed, **SHAME**, mortified, and in all honesty, just hoping it would all go away one day. Maybe there would be a miraculous healing, and no one would ever have to know. That was my prayer. I eventually drifted off to sleep. I was glad I finally released some of that bottled-up anxiety that had tormented me for months.

Lesson learned: Endurance

Endurance is *the ability to withstand hardship or adversity* defined by Merriam-Webster.com. Lesson learned, I survived! I mentioned laying in my bed in a fetal position. That position, along with wanting to pull my hair out, seemed to become a welcoming feeling that I experienced often. If I had known then what I know now, I would have searched for Christian Counseling until I found someone to meet with. I would not have hidden behind the embarrassment and got the help I needed. 2 Corinthians 4:17 says, *"For our light affliction, which is but for a moment, worketh for us a far more exceeding and eternal weight of glory."* I'm grateful to God for allowing me to go through what I did without losing my mind. He gets the glory out of this. The Bible also tells us in Matthew 24:13, *"But he that shall endure unto the end, the same shall be saved."*

Are you struggling with a crisis in your life that you feel you can't endure? Don't give up mid-stream. His word is true, and what He promises He will do. I encourage you to seek counsel. The resources are countless; there is someone somewhere who can lend a helping hand in your situation.

CHAPTER 4

Sunday Shock

Casting all your care upon him; for he careth for you.
- I Peter 5:7

Many people visited our home daily. Nurses, family, friends, people from church, and choir members rotated around the clock. Being the introvert I am, the number of people visiting and always trying to make sure the house was presentable for guests was totally wearing on my emotional and physical strength. I learned to grin and bear it for the sake of my husband. He grew weaker and weaker. It wasn't looking good at all. He was assigned a hospice nurse. They explained they wanted him to have services and that it wasn't necessarily a death sentence, but I knew it was a matter of time. Later that month, some choir members asked to come by and go over the details of the play I wrote. The Easter play *"He Decided to Die"* was scheduled for Good Friday. They arrived right after dinner, and we discussed some final changes to the play. After we finished, they asked if they could pray for my husband. I gladly responded, "Prayer is always welcome." They both kneeled beside the bed and began to pray with such fervor. We felt the almighty presence of God fill his bedroom. My husband laid quietly in the bed with his eyes closed and a smile of contentment on his face. They didn't stay long. They completed the task for the evening, said goodbye, and left. Something about the rest of the evening and later that night felt different. A calmness came over him that I hadn't witnessed in all the weeks he had been home. It felt as if a wave of peace had swept through our home. I retired for the evening, although I was unable to sleep. I laid in my bed staring at the ceiling, mesmerized by the spinning of each blade of the ceiling fan, wondering what the next day would bring.

It was Sunday morning, and like clockwork, the nurse came for her usual visit. For some reason, I chose not to go to church that morning. His godmother decided also to stay home that day. The nurse did her normal routine, checked his vitals, tried to get him to eat some breakfast, and administered his meds. He had no appetite; by this time, most meals consisted of half a glass of Ensure. She asked him, "How are you feeling?" and he responded, "I'm cold." She whispered to me, "His body temperature is a little cooler than normal." In my mind, I knew what that meant but was too afraid to ask any further questions. She sat quietly with him as I tended to things around the house, trying to keep busy. After a couple of hours, she did one final check of his vitals, gathered her belongings told him, "I'll see you next Sunday." The rest of the day, he slept. I decided to warm some leftover chicken and green beans and add a spoonful of potato salad for me and his godmother to eat. As we finished, I heard a knock at the door. My parents came by after leaving their church services to check on us. My mother asked, "How are you all doing?" and I responded, "About the same." They debated whether to stay or leave. I insisted they go home, eat dinner, get comfortable, and maybe return later. They hesitated but took my advice and headed out the door.

Still trying to keep busy, I decided to wash the dinner plates and clean up the kitchen. While working in the kitchen, I heard weak sounds coming from the room where he was. I walked in and found him awake. I asked him if he wanted to try and eat something. He never verbally responded but shook his head no. Since he was awake, his godmother and I seized the moment to reminisce about things in the past. He was the president of our youth choir, so we talked about singing engagements, rehearsals, and out-of-town trips, hoping that he would remember something and join in on the conversation. His voice was very shallow, and he barely said a word despite the stories we shared. We could tell he knew what we were talking about by his frequent smiles. Although he laid quietly listening to us, we could tell he was trying to say something. To our surprise, he managed to blurt out again, "I'm cold." Even though I had several blankets at the house, I asked his godmother if she would mind me making a quick run to the nearby Target to buy him a new blanket. She looked a little surprised but could feel that it was something that I wanted to do and agreed to stay while I made the quick run. I drove in the car in silence. No radio, no CDs, just total silence. I began to talk to the Lord, reminding Him what His word told me in 1 Peter 5:7, *"Casting all your care upon him; for he careth for you."* Repeating to myself, for He careth for me, for He careth for me. It was as if I was trying to remind the Lord or, better yet, question Him, "You really do care for me, Lord, don't you?" I swiftly ran into the store, found what I thought was the perfect navy-blue soft fleece blanket, and rushed back home in what seemed like 15 minutes. By the time I returned, his eyes were closed, and his breathing didn't seem normal at all. There was a look on his godmother's face that frightened me. I wondered what had happened in just the short time that I had been gone. She didn't say a word to me but began to talk to him to try and get him to respond, to no avail. It was time for our weekly church radio broadcast, so I grabbed my radio/alarm clock from my bedroom and plugged it into the socket in the room where he was. After what seemed like a long day, we were glad to hear the sound of the melodious voices of the choir. We all listened attentively as the choir sang their first song and then the second one. The prayer list was announced, and we heard his name called. Within minutes the pastor stated his normal greeting, "Jesus, the Light of the World." I asked him if he knew who that was, and he nodded and scarcely whispered the pastor's name. It became very quiet in the room, only the sound of the pastor asking anyone who desired prayer to call the prayer line. Within a matter of seconds, his godmother and I heard a loud gasp. We looked at each other in astonishment and knew he had taken his last breath. She looked at me and said, "He's gone." She informed me that it seemed like he was fading away while I was gone, but she begged him to hold on until I got back. That explained the pale look on her face when I returned. Even though I knew it was inevitable, I was not prepared at all. I was lost for words. What I thought would one day happen was now a reality.

I ran out of the room and landed in the hallway leaning against the wall. I felt all energy leave my body as I slid down the wall and plummeted flat on the floor, crying hysterically. His godmother ran out of the room to console me. She embraced me and just held me as I sobbed. As I pulled myself together, she said we needed to call the church. I told her, "No one will answer the phone during service." Then I remembered the prayer line. The broadcast was still on, so I knew someone was still manning the phone. I nervously dialed the number, and a familiar voice answered. The person that answered the phone recognized my voice. I told her while bitterly crying, "I just lost my husband." She responded by saying, "I'm so sorry." I asked her to make sure that she gave the news to the pastor and hung up the phone. Apparently, she went into the sanctuary and relayed the message. On the radio, I could hear disruptions in the background, realizing the news had made it to the choir, and then the broadcast went off. I was able to pull myself together to make a few more phone calls. I called the hospice nurse, and she advised, "I'm on my way. I'll call the funeral home. Do not worry about anything." I called my mother, and she and my father were at my front door within minutes, regretting leaving earlier that day. I called his sister to inform her to get to the house. Not being very far, she rushed over. I managed to go back into the room where he was but could not stand the sight. I resorted to my bedroom, buried my head in my clasped hands, and bawled. I eventually came out of my room to find a house full of people. My eyes were bloodshot, and my throat felt like a dry desert from all the crying. I sat in the living room, trying my best to keep my composure yet breaking down every time someone new came through the door, stating how sorry they were. People were everywhere, in the living room, dining room, the kitchen, and some even in the room with him. Finally, the funeral directors arrived, and my father told me, "You probably don't want to see them take him out, so why not go into your bedroom." I had mixed feelings but decided to follow his instructions. Several friends went in with me and consoled me as I heard them pass my door and exit out the front door. I could only imagine the sight of a black bag with my husband's remains leaving the house, never to return. By this time, my head felt as if it was about to burst open. My introverted behavior was kicking in again, and all I wanted was for people to leave and let me process what had just happened. I wanted to go to bed and wake up from this dreaded nightmare. Unfortunately, it wasn't a dream. It was my reality, in living color.

Lesson learned: Faith

Faith — Well, Merriam-Webster did a fantastic job defining this word. *"Belief and trust in and loyalty to God, firm belief in something for which there is no proof."* In all honesty, my faith was shaken. I believed God would perform a miracle for the man I loved. Now I was left with everything I had built my life around for the past seven years totally erased from my vision board of life. Yes, I knew Hebrews 11:1 by heart, *"Now faith is the substance of things hoped for, the evidence of things not seen,"* but the things I'd hoped for didn't happen. I realize now that my faith was in action, and I wasn't even aware of it. It took faith for me just to get out of bed the morning after. It took faith to walk down that long aisle on the day of the funeral. It took faith to go back to work after a couple of weeks off. It took faith to tell myself I could do this. My faith was not in myself but in my Almighty Father, Jesus Christ, who brought me through.

Has your faith been tested? Are you struggling with trusting God for what seems impossible? I encourage you with Jeremiah 17:7, *"Blessed is the man that trusteth in the LORD, and whose hope the LORD is."* Put your trust in Jesus!

CHAPTER 5

The Promise

For your shame ye shall have double, and for confusion they shall rejoice in their portion: therefore in their land they shall possess the double: everlasting joy shall be unto them.
 - Isaiah 61:7

The night seemed endless. Everyone, including my parents, my pastor, and my close friends, wanted to spend the night with me or take me to their home. As grateful as I was to my husbands' godmother for staying with us from the time he came home from the hospital, I even wanted her to go home. Dealing with the **SHAME** of what had just taken place in my home increased my desire to be alone. I insisted on staying by myself that night. In the wee hours of the morning, I shut the door on the last person. I laid across the bed with a million thoughts and questions running through my head. Wow, it only takes a matter of seconds to go from a married woman to a single, unmarried widow. How do I go on? How do I go from two incomes to just one? Always living with someone, to now living alone? Was I really ready for what was ahead of me? Again, so many questions. Emotions were at an all-time high. I was angry with myself, God, and my husband. Myself for allowing me to be in this position. Again, asking why didn't I just leave. Angry at God for allowing me to go through this. Angry at my husband for the choices he made on the one hand, for hurting me and leaving me on the other hand. Anger became the predominant emotion I would fight for the next couple of years. Eventually, I managed to close my eyes and fall asleep for a couple of hours. The next morning, I arose to the sound of the phone ringing. Call after call, inquiring how I was doing and what did I need? Visits, calls, and delivery of various foods and drinks were welcomed over the next couple of days. Here I was again, just four months after my aunt's passing, preparing to visit another funeral home to make final arrangements. Sitting behind the desk across from an undertaker was not where I wanted to be. Overwhelming, to say the least! My husband's father, who was deceased at this time, during his lifetime owned a Funeral Home establishment and had worked with several funeral homes for years. Each time a family member died, the same funeral home handled the arrangements. We met with the funeral home on a sunny brisk March day. Even though the sun was shining, it appeared to be a melancholy gloomy day for me. Accompanied by my parents and my sister-in-law, we drove to what seemed like a long road trip to the facility that was only 20 minutes from my home. Others met us there to help with the process. As we pulled into the parking lot, the agony of the pain in my stomach seemed unbearable. Even though I was with family, I still felt that I was to present a strong front. I pulled myself together, inconspicuously wiped away the lone tear that escaped from my eye, and walked into this dreaded building frequently visited by many at one of the most difficult times in life. As we walked through the front door, we were greeted by soft music and the friendly smile of the receptionist who escorted us into a nearby office. Even though I had encountered this process with others, this was my first time in the driver's seat. Decisions, decisions. First things first, what date for the services? We were entering the week of Easter. I didn't want the funeral to be on Good Friday because I didn't want that day to be a constant annual reminder of the day that changed my life. Along with his sister's consent, we decided to have the wake on Wednesday and the funeral on Thursday morning of the same week. We completed most of the paperwork and received a lot of perks because of the relationship with his father's funeral home. Finally, it was time for the unimaginable. The funeral director looked me in the eye and stated, "We're about to go into the room to select the casket. Are you ready?" A repeat of the pain I felt in my stomach just a few minutes earlier had resurfaced. With much hesitation and a shallow voice, I answered, "I think so." We walked together to the basement of the building. As we entered the room, someone was holding me by the arm, but I was in shock; I had no idea who it was. Caskets were everywhere. I literally lost it. It felt like all the energy in my body evaporated like a vapor into thin air. A loud scream and the tears that raced down my face together sent everyone rushing to console me. By this time, it seemed everyone was crying. I quickly pulled myself together and repeated to myself, "I can do this; I can do this." I told my sister-in-law, "Let's do this so we can go." After a totally exhausting experience, we finished and returned home to rest for the remainder of the day.

Unfortunately, resting was not on the agenda. With the funeral scheduled for three days later, there was so much to do. He was gifted a new navy suit that he had never worn, never even imagining what the actual outcome of that gift would be. I had to search for something for me to wear, a navy suit, and of course, many necessary appointments to prepare for the wake and the service. Visitors still bombarded my house each day and night. It was finally the evening of the wake. I got dressed, pulled out that imaginary mask to hide my true feelings, and tried to manage what was going on in my stomach with a glass of hot tea. I was escorted to the funeral home for the first viewing.

My sister-in-law, my parents, other family members, and I walked into the room with a sense of calmness as we saw the casket and the beautiful display of flowers. The closer we got to the casket and saw his body lying there, my emotions intensified. As my heart rate increased to an all-time high, reality hit me; my husband was lying in a casket before me. I am a widow, and my husband died of AIDS. I was seated in the front row pew, where someone handed me a tissue to wipe the tears streaming down my face. I sat in silence as visitors began filling the room fighting the **SHAME** of why we were even here and wondering what people thought as they viewed his body. As the evening went on, I successfully greeted the many people who came to support me, desperately wanting it all to end.

The day of the funeral was extremely difficult. I struggled between two emotions, grief and **SHAME,** and couldn't figure out which was predominant. I wanted to hold it all together the best I could but realized that was utterly impossible. I thought the evening before was extremely hard, and what on earth was about to happen today? I got up early because I figured it would take me a while to prepare myself for the day and get dressed. I tried my best to eat a light breakfast, but each bite of food I swallowed felt as if it was coming back up. Later my family arrived, and we all waited for the funeral home limousine to pick us up.

While riding to the church in the limousine, I tried to focus on simply just getting through the day. Music was playing in the vehicle, and I hadn't really paid attention to it until we got about a mile from the church. I heard the lyrics, *"And when I'm gone, please carry on. Don't cry for me."* Was this a message for me? Well, if so, it didn't work. Tears began to roll down my face, and my ability to hold it together was a total wash. We lined up, me in the front. I walked down the aisle with my parents on both sides, feeling as if everyone was whispering, "I told you so." Trying dreadfully to hide the **SHAME** I was feeling. Many people had great things to say about my husband, but it wasn't until my dear friend sang my requested song, *"Faith that Conquers Anything,"* that I felt a release. As she melodiously belted out, "Faith that can conquer anything," I felt a move of God overtake me. It was an assurance that I had made it this far by Faith and that Faith would carry me for the rest of this journey. I managed to make it through the rest of the service and even to the burial grounds.

The next day was Good Friday and the day of the play, *"He Decided to Die."* It was dedicated to the memory of my husband. Many family members came out to witness the production as well as to support me. The play was phenomenal, depicting the events leading to the crucifixion of Jesus Christ. It was a great way to end an overwhelmingly stressful week.

Even though my pastor and his wife were a strong support to me during this time, I had not shared my story with them. I realized it was past time to sit and talk with him. I met with him and told him everything I had been going through since the day I found out. I asked him, "Who am I?" I told him I felt **SHAME** had stolen my identity and didn't know who I was anymore. He told me, "You are a child of God created in his image, and God loves you more than you realize." He sat and cried with me and then prayed for me. His words were a comfort to me, "Daughter, I love you, and you will be all right!"

Easter Sunday, I decided I would go to church in spite of the fact I had no desire. I was physically, mentally, and emotionally exhausted. I got up that morning, moving slowly. I thought I must look good today; that would take the attention off the past few days. I dressed in a sharp, mint green suit adorned with beautiful gold buttons and drove to church. The feeling of loneliness gripped my very being. I thought church was the best thing for me; however, when I walked through the door, a feeling of total **SHAME** overtook me to the point that I wanted to sink into the floor. The play was in the building across the street, so the last time I walked through the doors of the church, I was walking down the aisles with all eyes on me to my husband's services. I experienced that same deep feeling of **SHAME** I felt on Thursday at the funeral. I sat in the audience that Sunday, avoiding my usual seat in the choir stand, and allowed the tears to flow. I talked to myself through the entire service, "Granotta, pull yourself together. Granotta, you don't want people to see you like this. Granotta, you'll be fine; just make it through this service. Granotta, don't leave." I was so worried about what people thought of me. I was absorbed in **SHAME** so much that I wanted to get up and leave. However, I was afraid that would just draw more attention to me. The three-hour service seemed like six hours, but finally, I heard the preacher say amen. Trying to avoid as many people as possible was hopeless. It seemed everyone in the church wanted a piece of me; hugs, kisses, and those stating, "I'm sorry," kept me from making a beeline to the exit door. At last, I made it to my car. My first thought was to head home and hide in the warm covers of my bed, but my family insisted on gathering for our usual Easter Sunday dinner. By the time I arrived, I felt totally disoriented. I put that old familiar mask on. Yes, I also wore it around my family and endured all the attention I received from them. After all, it was only one week from the actual death of my husband. By the end of the gathering, I collected all my belongings, leftover food I knew I would never eat, and headed to my home alone. I nestled in my quiet home, realizing this was the new normal moving forward. Silent tears streaming down my face somehow turned into an uncontrollable sob. I began to cry out to the Lord, "I need your help! I can't do this by myself. I need to hear from you, Jesus!" Then I began to prepare myself for bed. As I was finishing up in the bathroom, I heard the phone ring but decided I didn't want to talk to anyone, and without checking the caller id, I ignored it. Evidently, the caller was persistent because shortly after the first call, the phone rang again. I then decided to check to see who it was. It was one of the evangelists from my church. Struggling to decide whether to answer, I reluctantly picked up the phone. She asked me how I was doing. Not one to freely open up to people, I simply responded, "I'm fine," knowing that was farthest from the truth. She questioned, "Are you sure about that?" I wanted to ask, what kind of question is that? I just lost and buried my husband, and you want to know how I'm doing. Realizing she wasn't going to get much out of me, she continued. With excitement in her voice, she stated, "Well, I have something to share with you that the Lord gave me." In my mind, I was thinking, ok, here we go, a word from the Lord. I could feel my eyeballs rolling in my head. She referred me to a scripture in the Bible and asked me to look it up. I wasn't at all in the mood for this, but being respectful, I grabbed my Bible and turned to Isaiah 61:7 as she instructed. With still amazement in her voice, she stated, read it. With an attitude, I read, *"For your shame ye shall have double, and for confusion they shall rejoice in their portion: therefore in their land they shall possess the double: everlasting joy shall be unto them."* Honestly, I almost collapsed in my own home all by myself. When I read the word **SHAME** and realized that was the very sentiment I had been feeling all along and especially at church, I began to cry uncontrollably. I wondered where that scripture had been hiding because I didn't remember ever reading it prior to that night. The hour-long conversation was exactly what I needed. With exhilaration in her voice, she questioned, "Do you believe God's promises are true? Do you realize who you are in Christ?" She answered her own questions by saying, "God's promises are true, and despite how bad you feel, God will get the glory out of this situation." We hung up the phone with me rejoicing, feeling thankful to God for this incredible woman who mentored and walked beside me the many days ahead during this difficult test.

The next day I called the evangelist and told her what a blessing she was to me. She had such a strong faith in God and became such an instrument in helping me. I could call her anytime, day or night, whether I was having a good or bad day. Many times, she would share a word or scripture to ease whatever emotion I was dealing with that day. The scripture she shared with me that evening was etched in my spirit and became the foundation of what God had in store for me. He promised He would take away the **SHAME** and give me DOUBLE!

Lesson Learned: Assurance

Assured —is, according to Merriam-Webster, *sure that something is certain or true*. Sometimes when we feel all hope is gone, God has a way of letting us know that he says what he means, and he means what he says. Even though I really didn't want to talk to the evangelist who called me, what she shared with me was exactly what I needed at that very moment. God used her to allow me to see things in a different light. I felt a sense of hope I hadn't felt in a long time. At that moment, I was in a very good place. The scripture that encouraged me was Philippians 4:8, "*Finally, brethren, whatsoever things are true, whatsoever things are honest, whatsoever things are just, whatsoever things are pure, whatsoever things are lovely, whatsoever things are of good report; if there be any virtue, and if there be any praise, think on these things."* I had no idea what double meant or how it would manifest in my life, but I trusted God. I was assured that what he said he would do would be done. It all began with a change in my mind.

Think of one thing that you can believe God for. What are your true thoughts about that situation? Do you have positive thoughts, or do you doubt yourself or even God? Change your thought process and your attitude about the struggle. Then watch God work.

CHAPTER 6

What about me?

And the peace of God, which passeth all understanding, shall keep your hearts and minds through Christ Jesus.
- Philippians 4:7

The funeral, the play, Easter Sunday, and all the emotions that came with each day were now behind me. Everyone returned to their homes, and I chose to be left alone. "Me time" was a way of life. So much to process. My state of mind was hard to figure out. I couldn't really determine what I was dealing with. I was dealing with grief but added a new emotion, fear. Fear of the unknown. Yes, I wanted to grieve the death of a spouse like most people; however, anger and distress were overriding me as well. Which was predominant? I couldn't tell. At this time, AIDS was all over the news. It appeared on almost every news channel, and several newspapers had information on the threat of this disease. To make matters worse, headlines emphasized how women were dying of AIDS at a rapid rate. According to the Centers for Disease Control and Prevention, *HIV infection was the second leading cause of death for black women aged 25-44 (up from third in 1991) in 1992.* I was 35 at the time and fell right in the middle of that age range. Inevitably I had to get tested, but the very thought of it left me shaking frantically in my boots. I would put it off month after month, rationalizing that I was fine and did not want to deal with the **SHAME** of the doctor's visit. I had no known symptoms, so what was the rush? How insanely crazy that was! But that's how I dealt with a lot of circumstances at that time. "Just ignore it if possible and deal with it at my convenience." At a loss for words, I prayed, and the only thing I could utter was, "God, Please Help Me!" Finally, several months later, my pastor pulled me over, checking on me as he occasionally did. He inquired, "Daughter, how are you getting along?" The next statement that came out of his mouth threw me for a loop. He whispered, "Have you been tested yet?" I whispered back to him, "No, sir." He bucked his eyes at me and said, "What are you waiting for? You know you must get it done." Just the conversation bought so much anxiety, and yes, again, **SHAME**. He made me promise to make an appointment and offered to drive me. As difficult as it was, I kept my promise. I was working during the day, so making that call presented a challenge for me. I surely did not want anyone to hear me on the phone, so I decided to wait until I could take a break and go to my car for privacy. I called my doctor and requested an appointment. The receptionist asked, "And for what reason are you needing an appointment." With tears rolling down my face, I apprehensively uttered the words, "I need an AIDS test." The sudden change in the receptionist's voice made me feel so **ASHAMED,** as if she could see me through the telephone. She scheduled me for the following week. Upset stomach, restlessness, tension, tiredness, sleepless nights, and trouble concentrating settled in with me the week before my visit. I decided to take the day off to focus on what I had to do that day and how I would get through it. Despite my pastor's invitation to go with me, I chose to go alone. I drove in silence, wondering why am I going through this. How did I get here? As I pulled into the parking lot, I looked in the mirror to wipe away the flood of tears from my eyes. I walked into a waiting room that was full of patients waiting to be seen by the doctor. A whirlwind of thoughts raced through my mind. I checked in and waited patiently for my turn. As my name was called, I gathered my belongings and steadied myself to hide the weakness in my knees I felt walking from the chair to the door. The routine checkup of my weight and blood pressure seemed so unnecessary at the time. All I wanted was to get the test over and get out of there. When the doctor entered my room, she found me tensely sitting, twilling my thumbs. She asked several questions and then addressed my reason for visiting her. Her first question was, "When were you exposed?" I explained, "My husband died from AIDS several months ago." With dismay in her eyes, she asked, "Why did you wait so long to get tested?" I simply said, "It's hard to explain." She replied, "Normally, a test is administered six months after initial contact and then another six months after that. Since you are already in excess of the six-month time frame, if the test returns negative, you are most likely ok, but I'll still do the second test." What a sigh of relief. Even though I had no results yet, I felt pretty good about the visit. She ordered complete blood work, which I had to have at another clinic. I felt a burst of energy and drove straight to the clinic to do the test.

The nurse advised me that the results would take three to five days. My pastor, my parents, and a few friends were aware of what I was doing and were all praying for me. After a few days, one early evening, I received a phone call. The voice on the other end stated calmly, "Hello, this is your doctor's office calling you with your test results." I thought at first it must be bad news for them to call that late in the day. She went through what seemed like a long list of results stating everything was fine, and the last thing stated, "Your AIDS test is negative." I wanted to run laps around my neighborhood. I began to thank the Lord for what He had done for me. As indicated, I took the second test six months later, received a negative diagnosis, and was told I would not have to take it again. All the months of living with AIDS had finally come to an end. I no longer had to worry about myself. By the grace of God, wondering if I had contracted AIDS was now a thing of the past.

What a relief. Physically I was a walking miracle. Mentally, a different story. I kept hearing the scripture in my mind, "*And the peace of God, which passeth all understanding, shall keep your hearts and minds through Christ Jesus.*" Philippians 4:7. I desired peace but struggled daily to maintain it. I felt my mind was by no means being kept on any level. I wanted everyone to think I was getting stronger and stronger as each day passed; however, that was far from the truth. I sensed that my mental stability would eventually crumble before my very eyes. I needed help! I started off by going back to my same primary doctor. I was suffering from changes in sleeping habits, no energy, feeling lonely, constant sadness, and no appetite, to name a few. After asking me an array of questions, she concluded, "You're dealing with depression, and rightfully so, with all you've been through." Without hesitation, she wrote a prescription for Prozac. Just like that! That was not my expectation! I thought, "Shouldn't I speak to a psychologist or psychiatrist first?" I reluctantly took the prescription to Walgreens and waited for them to fill it. I never wanted to take medication to make me feel better and was so fearful of unknown side effects. While my symptoms continued, I decided to try it after a few days. I took one pill on the first day and repeated it on the second day. After the second attempt, I felt my heart racing, and as if my head spun at 90 miles an hour. What I was feeling I knew I didn't like and decided then not to take any more of that medication. Unfortunately, I still was unable to sleep. I began taking over-the-counter sleeping aids. It first started out once or twice a week and soon increased as needed. Eventually, I was totally dependent on those sleeping pills to rock me to sleep every night. What a trick of the enemy. I refused to take Prozac but relied heavenly on another form of addictive medication. I refused to let the enemy in through the front door but opened the window for easy access. This went on for months. I resorted to calling my doctor to address the matter at hand. I stated to her, "I'm not comfortable at all with this medication." She responded, "I want you to see a therapist, and I'll send you a list of my recommendations." Once I received the list, I decided to take a week off work. I needed a therapist, so I began researching the candidates. I chose a female therapist, thinking she would understand my feelings from a woman's perspective. I made the appointment and went to the first visit. I toiled with so many emotions on that first visit. Just the thought of having to talk to a psychologist intimidated me. It didn't help that her office was in the same hospital that my husband was in. That brought back so many memories of what seemed like endless visits to that facility. We talked for the entire 60 minutes, primarily answering questions she posed. After about the third visit, I realized that going to this room on the 19th floor of the hospital made me feel like something was wrong with me. My insurance covered me for ten visits, but by the eighth visit, I decided this was enough. Unfortunately, Christian counselors were not as much of an option as they are today, so she and I disagreed on several issues. I questioned myself, what have I gained from these eight visits? I did discover that, all along, I had blamed myself for all that I had experienced. She convinced me that none of it was my fault and that had my husband been married to any other woman, the outcome would have been the same. No Prozac, no counseling, still trapped in sleeping pills. What next? I lost all confidence in counseling and did not seek any further assistance in that area. I decided the best way to deal with what was going on in my mind was to keep busy.

I remained involved at my church, continuing to work as a choir director and Sunday School teacher and serving with the women's ministry. Outside of church, I started a children's Bible study ministry at a foster home. Each week I would visit the children in the foster home and share with them the love of Jesus. Something they weren't privy to in their day-to-day environment. Whatever reason landed them in an institutionalized facility, I was determined to let them know how much they were loved. I made it my business to include love in every single lesson. It was important to me that even if they knew nothing else, they would know I brought love to them on a silver platter when they saw me coming. I grew so attached to them that I would frequently take a child home with me for the weekend and over Christmas break. All ages, the kids would be so excited to see me every Tuesday evening as I arrived. I developed a love for those kids who, through their own innocence, were left alone without the love of a mommy or daddy. While helping them the best I could, those precious babies had no idea how much they were helping me. What a healing; being able to ease the pain and spread the love of Jesus was a balm for my own scars. After all, I didn't have to hide **SHAME** from these children. That experience sparked a desire for me to one day become an adoptive parent. It hurt my heart to see so many children longing to be loved, yet no one to open their hearts or homes to them. Even though Tuesday evenings were so refreshing, it seemed the joy I felt was left there as I drove home each week. I continued trying my best to function as normally as I could but knew there was still a missing link. I couldn't quite put my finger on it, but I still desired to be free from the sleeping pills and loneliness, and most of all, I desired peace. So, what did I do? I drove home each week, prepared for the next day, filled my glass of water, placed it on my nightstand, took my sleeping pills, and fell asleep.

It took months for me to realize that I was actually addicted. One Sunday, while in church, I was standing up in the choir stand, and I noticed a sister in the audience who seemed to be staring at me. Unlike me, a lifelong member of the church, she had joined a few years prior, but I really didn't know her. The look on her face was as if she saw something strange. I looked away and paid no attention to her, but as I glanced back in her direction, I noticed she had the same look on her face and was still staring directly at me. I dismissed it and went about my business. Later that day, before the evening service, I met her unexpectedly face to face. She hesitated but politely asked me, "Can I talk to you?" Curious as to why she was staring at me earlier that day, I answered, "Sure." She enquired, "Did you see me staring at you during service this morning?" I responded, "Yes, I did. What was that about?" The look I saw on her face during the service seemed to resurface as she stated, "I saw in the spirit that your face was very distorted; it appeared all twisted and out of shape." She continued advising me, "The enemy is out to destroy you, BUT God has a hedge around you, and He will fulfill His purpose in you." She said that at first, she didn't want to tell me, but she told the Lord if it was His will to allow our paths to cross that day, she would do it. God did it. I knew it was God that sent her to talk to me. I felt comfortable sharing with her things I hadn't shared with anyone else. I told her about the Prozac prescription, the sleeping pills, and the therapist visits. I stressed how **SHAME** had a stronghold on me, and I felt it was wrecking my life. She encouraged me not to allow the enemy to destroy me and to know without a doubt that God was with me. She asked if she could pray with me. I agreed, and the power of God fell upon me that evening. This time tears of joy streamed down my face instead of tears of sadness. I felt the presence of God that I had desperately longed for and, yes, that peace that passeth understanding that I strongly desired.

I went home that night, fighting the enemy the entire drive. He wanted me to believe that when it was time to go to bed, I would reach for the sleeping pills. Well, he was right; I grabbed the pills and flushed them down the toilet. I was done! Dressed in my cozy pajamas, I nestled in my bed and fell fast asleep. What the enemy meant for evil, God turned around. I knew this was an extraordinary turning point for me. The excitement overtook me, and I felt a huge smile on my face. I couldn't wait to express my joy to my family. I scheduled a breakfast meeting with my parents, my four siblings, and their spouses and shared my life's journey thus far, including how God used this sister to let me know He was still with me. Once again, because of **SHAME**, this was the first time I openly talked to my family about this difficult journey I had been on for months. The fact that I had so much good news made it so much easier.

Lesson learned: Protection

The verb protect is defined by dictionary.com as *"to defend or guard from attack, invasion, loss, annoyance, insult, etc.; cover or shield from injury or danger."* I knew women who died from being exposed to someone that was infected with AIDS; therefore, I knew that it was the grace of God that kept me alive and healthy. He had angels watching over me. I should have been a statistic, but the mercies of God kept me. I lived by Psalm 91:11, *"For he shall give his angels charge over thee, To keep thee in all thy ways."* Angels kept me from contracting AIDS, from continual reliance on sleeping pills, from losing my mind, and so much more. I can't thank God enough for keeping me. Through the years, I have learned that God keeps us when we don't want to be kept or when we don't deserve to be kept. Even when we don't realize that He's keeping us, He's doing it! What a merciful

God. I dare you to take a moment and think of a time when you know God protected you. Or maybe you're feeling unprotected as if you're all alone. Stand on His promises and what His word says. There is assurance in the Psalms:

> *"The Lord shall preserve thy going out and thy coming in from this time forth, and even for evermore." -* ***Psalm 121:8***

> *"God is our refuge and strength, a very present help in trouble."*
> *-* ***Psalm 46:1***

> *"The righteous cry, and the Lord heareth, and delivereth them out of all their troubles. The Lord is nigh unto them that are of a broken heart; and saveth such as be of a contrite spirit."*
> *-* ***Psalm 34: 17-18***

CHAPTER 7

The Aftermath

And be ye kind one to another, tenderhearted, forgiving one another, even as God for Christ's sake hath forgiven you.
- Ephesians 4:32

My high of being free from sleeping pills, talking to my family, and, most importantly, experiencing the peace of God revitalized my very being. Examining myself, I realized I had one more thing to do in order to maintain my state of being. I had to deal with the F word: FORGIVENESS. As stated, I did not sit before a Christian counselor; therefore, a lot of our views conflicted. Not one time was the word forgiveness ever mentioned in any of the sessions. Being in church all my life, I had heard many sermons on forgiveness, but living and acting upon it, I can't say this was something I had experienced. After all, how do you forgive someone who is no longer on the face of the Earth? I had a real problem with that. One would ask, didn't you know something wasn't right? Didn't you notice unusual behaviors? Well, here's where I thought forgiveness had taken place. I had heard things in the past, but when a person tells

SHAME ON ME—NO MORE!

you that God has delivered them and now their desire was to put the past behind them and move on, I found myself believing them. After all, he said he loved me and would do anything for me, and he was in the church, loved by everyone. What more could you ask for? Yes, I loved him. But now it was different. I had a choice, live my life in bondage or choose the process of forgiveness. It wasn't easy. For me, all I wanted to do was give the person who harmed me a piece of my mind and deal with forgiveness later. I deeply wanted to tell him every ounce of what I had experienced and how his actions hurt me so deeply. But again, utterly impossible since he was no longer here. I began a long journey of studying forgiveness. I visited Christian bookstores searching for books, read my Bible, and listened to sermons on cassette tapes. They were all a part of my pursuit of answers to this dilemma.

One day while driving out of town for my job, I was listening to the radio. I decided I wanted to hear some inspiring words and put the radio on scan since I wasn't familiar with the area stations. Finally, I heard a station that sounded as if it would satisfy my desires. I hit the button to stop the scanning, and the voice on the radio was a pastor. The next words out of his mouth were, "To forgive is as if the offense never happened." I thought, what on earth did I just hear? Definitely something that did not resonate with me at all. I quickly changed the station and began listening to music. I tried to drown the thought out by singing the song now playing, but that thought simmered in my head the rest of the day. In my mind, this was insanely impossible. No one has any idea what I have gone through, the **SHAME**, hurt, pain, loneliness, and heartache, and I'm supposed to act as if it never happened?! "No way, Jose." Let's table this. I remained in a state of bondage for years because I chose not to forgive. In hindsight, what a terrible place to be. If only I had realized that I was only hurting myself. See, unforgiveness never hurts the person causing the harm but will do damage to your very being. I would often be in services or revivals and would be called out by the preacher who would pray over me. In most cases, they would reference something about my past. It seemed I was a target each time I attended a service. I questioned myself. What does forgiveness entail, and how would I know if I had actually forgiven him? At this point, I still wasn't able to talk openly about it or even entertain the thought of sharing my story with anyone. Yes, **SHAME** hadn't gone anywhere. It was still hounding me. I eventually used that as a measuring stick. As soon as I felt I could talk about it and not feel remorse, hurt, or distress, I knew I had crossed over the bridge of forgiveness.

Months possibly years, flew by without me even thinking of the pact I made with myself until one year, while at a women's retreat, I experienced an unexpected release. Each year for several years, I attended a women's retreat held in a beautiful resort surrounded by mountains. A place I looked forward to visiting every year because I always felt that it was my time to experience a refreshing of God's spirit and enjoy the beautiful scenery of blue skies, mountain tops, and fresh air. One year at the close of the retreat, we were all gathered in the cozy meeting room to prepare to leave. The sister in charge stood before all of us and asked, "Does anyone have anything to share with the ladies before we leave?" Several sisters stood up and gave praises to God for deliverance over personal things they had been dealing with. I clearly heard the spirit speak to me and say, "You are free; stand up and tell your story." I sat there wondering, should I, should I not? I fought hard, and **SHAME** tried harder, but I managed to break loose. It was almost time to leave, and the sister said, "Is there anybody else?" I stood, and I proclaimed. "I thank God for victory. Today I'm free. My husband died of AIDS, and I've walked in unforgiveness and **SHAME** for years. But today, I am free." The sisters in the room began to clap with thunderous praise with me. I sat down and felt my shackles released. That was the first time in years that I could say aloud that my husband had AIDS. Of course, the enemy began to talk to me and say, "Look what you've done. People will start talking about you." Who are you fooling? These women don't know me and won't even see me anymore. I refused to give in to the thoughts battling in my head. I knew I felt something I had sought for years: FREEDOM. As we left the room and headed to our cars, three different women came to me with similar testimonies and thanked me for sharing just that small portion of my story. That's when I was sure I had done the right thing.

Many years later, I was at another women's retreat, this time amongst my own church members. The scenario was almost the same. We were at the end of the retreat, and due to a delay in the bus picking us up, we gathered outside and began to share how God had blessed us during this retreat. The title of the retreat was "I Survive." Once again, I felt the spirit of God tugging on me to share my story. I thought in my mind, "No way, this experience happened decades ago. No one wants to hear this." I waited patiently, sister after sister, got up and shared. Finally, I raised my hand, "I have a story. The theme of this retreat is I survive, but my story is I Survived!" The next words that flew out of my mouth were, "My first husband had," I stuttered and then continued, "No, I can say it, died of AIDS." A second release!! Sisters began to hug me, and one sister said everyone knew about him and there was no reason for you to live all those years in **SHAME**. Even though I knew I was free up in the mountains, I felt even better and had no doubt that I had truly put my past behind me. **SHAME ON ME NO MORE!**

Lesson learned: Forgiveness

The King James Bible Dictionary defines the word forgive as "*to pardon; to remit, as an offense or debt; to overlook an offense and treat the offender as not guilty.*" What in the world? Is that not what I heard the preacher say on the radio that I chose to ignore? We really don't realize the bondage that unforgiveness has over us. It can cause physical harm to our bodies, destroy us mentally and play tricks on our emotions. Once we realize the stronghold it has on us, it behooves us to get rid of it by any means necessary. Stop the revenge game. The Bible says in Romans 12:19, "*Dearly beloved, avenge not yourselves, but rather give place unto wrath: for it is written, Vengeance is mine, I will repay, saith the Lord.*" We have to take our hands off of it and let the Lord handle the offender. The reward is priceless. Our Father forgives us and expects us to forgive, as stated in Ephesians 4:32, "*and be ye kind one to another, tenderhearted, forgiving one another, even as God for Christ's sake hath forgiven you.*"

Who in your life do you need to forgive? The offender can be someone who personally hurt you, your child, or a family member, or even as difficult as someone who murdered someone close to you. No matter the offense, you've got to forgive. Some say it's a process; for others, it's not as difficult. The key is to do as Elsa in the movie Frozen, *"Let it Go!"* Believe me; it is possible to be free. According to Galatians 5: 1, *"Stand fast therefore in the liberty wherewith Christ hath made us free, and be not entangled again with the yoke of bondage."* Unforgiveness is a yoke of bondage that has the potential to choke the life out of us, but we have an option. I encourage you to choose freedom!

CHAPTER 8

I'm Available

Not that I speak in respect of want: for I have learned, in whatsoever state I am, therewith to be content. **- Philippians 4:11**

Was the desire to be married haunting me? Or should I have accepted the fact that just maybe I'll remain single the rest of the days of my life? I couldn't really figure it out. I thought, who would want a woman who was married to a man who died of AIDS? Who would even think twice about talking to me, dating me, or even loving me? I wrestled with the idea of getting used to this life all alone. I remained in the house my husband and I purchased prior to his death. Many lonely days and nights were my norm. Hanging out with some dear girlfriends on a regular basis was appreciated, and I much enjoyed their company, but still, I struggled with a deep feeling of being alone. Loneliness was real, and all the band-aids I used to cover up the scar did not heal the womb. Let's just be real: some days were good days, but it seemed most were extremely bad. I still fought depression, low self-esteem, and sleepless nights but refused the very thought of resorting back to any type of medication. There were times when I would tell myself, "Girl, you have every right to feel this way; after all, you have been through a very traumatic experience." In order to fight those feelings, talking to myself, encouraging myself, talking to my heavenly father, and reading His word became extremely necessary.

Being around married couples was a thorn in my flesh. Attending weddings was a challenge. Even being in the company of my siblings was tremendously upsetting because they were all married, and I was the only single one. Here I thought things would get better after his death, not realizing a whole new set of issues was on the horizon. Trying to accept this new way of life wasn't easy because deep down, I desired companionship. In reality, I missed my husband, and the thought of starting to date again caused me to gag. Of course, the first thought was, what if I ran into someone with the same history as my husband? Will I be able to spot anything unusual? I was in my late thirties and had just decided that most men my age were either already married, if single, settled into a life of being single, or just not interested in women, if you know what I mean. Then, of course, there was the should I, would I, could I, tell my story. Did I owe it to anyone to reveal the secrets of my past? Nah, unless I became serious with someone, my secret was safe with me. Opportunities arose when I went out and met people. Nothing significant, just a nice occasional dinner and maybe a movie. The conversations were great, and I welcomed the friendship.

One day I decided to share my story with a guy I had frequently spent time with. I really didn't care if the relationship developed into more than friendship, so I thought I would put it to the test. We went to a movie and then had dinner at a casual restaurant. After discussing the likes and dislikes of the movie and enjoying dessert, I started a new conversation by saying, "I have something to share with you." He asked, "Why such a serious look on your face?" So I continued, "There are some things about me that I don't readily share but just wanted to tell you." He listened attentively as I whispered, not wanting anyone else in the restaurant to hear me, "My husband died of AIDS." I waited patiently for his response behind the solemn look on his face. To my surprise, he wasn't moved by it. He asked me, "Are you ok?" I responded, "Oh yes." He continued by saying, "Despite the choices your husband made, thank God you are fine." A sign of relief. It made me feel a sense of acceptance. It erased the thought of rejection from the opposite sex because of my past. I felt the ideas were thoughts I had conjured up in my head. I sensed there was definitely hope for me in the dating and marrying spectrum. I had a ray of confidence that God did have someone for me, and all I needed to do was make myself "Available."

One morning I was lying in my warm bed, waiting for the alarm clock to go off. Needless to say, I had been toiling all week with the desire to get married again. Being single was not working for me, and I desperately wanted to remarry. My digital alarm played CDs, and you could set whatever song you wanted to be awakened to. I had just purchased the musical soundtrack of Bishop TD Jakes, Women Thou Art Loosed. My favorite song, and the most played on the CD, was *What a Mighty God We Serve*. It was my special song that blasted every morning to wake me up. I had not listened to the other songs because I was stuck on that one. As the clock struck 6:30, the sound of the music caught me off guard. I sat up and looked at the CD, wondering what track was playing. It surely wasn't the usual track 8. I listened to the intro and thought ok, who changed the song? How did the CD player get to track number 10 instead of my jam track number 8? I checked the title of the song. To my amazement, it was *I am your first husband.* I was flabbergasted! I could not believe what my ears were hearing. I settled myself and quietly listened to the words as tears streamed down my face. The leader of the song began with these words:

> *You want to be loved*
> *Let me love you,*
> *For I know you've been hurt*
> *So many times, before*
> *It's you and me*
> *Against adversity*
> *All I want*
> *Is to see you whole*
> *And complete*
> *I'm your closest friend*
> *I'll never leave you alone*
> *I'll be with you til the end*
> *Even when things go wrong*
> *Jesus said let me hold you in my arms*
> *Because I'm your first husband*

I could not contain myself. I could literally feel my father in heaven wrapping his arms around me. I was crying so hard I had to put the song on pause to make a run to the bathroom. I grabbed the box of tissue to blow my nose and wipe my face. Wanting to hear the rest of the song, I walked back into the bedroom, pressed play, and the chorus of the song put me right back where I was with the verse, bawling again.

There's no problem too hard
That I cannot solve
The childhood pain you can stop carrying
It wasn't yours
Let's look toward the future
Without fear of the past
I won't hold it against you
So receive my love at last
I am your first husband

I am your first love
I am your first love
I am your first love
I am your first husband

I continued rejoicing, feeling God had met me just where I was. It got even better; that wasn't all He had in store for me that morning. I finally got up to get dressed for work. As I was preparing to walk out the door, my phone rang. I said hello, but the voice on the other end was someone I didn't recognize, so I politely asked, "Who am I speaking with." It was a friend that had moved out of town and whom I hadn't spoken with in years. I have no idea how she even got my phone number. She said, "The Lord put you on my mind this morning, and I began praying for you." She continued, "And I want to share this scripture with you. Isaiah 54:5, *"For thy Maker is thine husband; the LORD of hosts is his name; and thy Redeemer the Holy One of Israel; The God of the whole earth shall he be called."* No words! I imagined the neighbors across the street could hear me crying and rejoicing about how God confirmed that He had me. I shared the alarm clock story with her; she praised God with me and ended the conversation in prayer. I no longer questioned God. I knew He would surely send someone searching for me in His time, and my past would not be an issue for them.

Lesson learned: Contentment

The dictionary defines contented as *a feeling or showing satisfaction with one's possessions, status, or situation.* Paul tells us in Philippians 4:11, *"Not that I speak in respect of want: for I have learned, in whatsoever state I am, therewith to be content."* Well, Paul, for some of us, this may not be easy. Many times, we find ourselves in situations, let's be real, that we just don't want to be in, and it is very hard to find contentment and peace. Looking back, I think of the hymn What a friend we have in Jesus. The words, *"Oh what peace we often forfeit, oh what needless pain we bear, all because we do not carry, everything to God in prayer,"* are so true and befitting, and if I would have only done as I Peter 5:7 tells us, *"Casting all your care upon him; for he careth for you,"* life would have been so much easier. Whatever your struggle is, first and foremost, Trust God, give Him your care, and find contentment in your situation. Our Father cares so much for you and will walk with you through your storm.

CHAPTER 9

The Beginning of a Friendship

*A man that hath friends must shew himself friendly: and there is a friend that sticketh closer than a bother. - **Proverbs 18:24***

Even though I was assured that marriage was in my future, the outlook was pretty bleak. Overall, I had a pretty mundane life that consisted of working a nine-to-five job which allowed me to travel frequently, be absorbed in church activities at least four days a week, and hang out with the girls, my besties! No one at work, no one at church, and nowhere else to even meet anyone. This task seemed utterly impossible. But I had a praying father. Unbeknownst to me, my father shared with my family at one of our holiday gatherings how he had been praying for his two daughters. His prayer for my sister was for her and her husband to have a child and for me to be married again. Half the prayer was already answered. My sister and her husband welcomed their first son and their second child, a baby girl, when he shared this information with us. I thought maybe there was some hope in his daily prayers.

The Bible says, *"Whoso findeth a wife findeth a good thing, and obtaineth favour of the LORD,"* Proverbs 18:22. Was I in the right place to be found? In my mind, NO! Driving over the roadways for work allotted me hours to think about where I was in life. I decided I needed to change my prayer. No longer IF this is what you have for me, but, Lord, prepare me for who you have for me. I felt I had packed years of hurt, heartache, betrayal, low self-esteem, and so much more in my own personal oversized suitcase that desperately needed to be cleaned out. I didn't feel that I loved myself, so how could I allow someone to love me? Again, the same questions resurfaced: Who would want to marry someone who's shared a life with a husband who died of AIDS? Who would give me the time of day? Who would love me? The beautiful mask I created hiding MYSELF needed to be snatched off, but was I willing to go to that length? So many questions. I had many long conversations with my mentor, who talked to me, as many would say, until I was blue in the face. She reiterated over and over, "Child, you are beautiful in the eyes of God and in the eyes of some gentleman out there. Wait on the Lord." She always used the words repeatedly, "Watch what I say."

A few weeks passed, and I was still pondering this whole idea of remarrying. I settled on this prayer. "Lord, here I am again. I come to you broken and messed up. Only you can fix me. Since, not IF this is your will for me, I need you to send my husband to my church." Just like that. I shocked myself. Where did this come from? I called my mentor and shared with her this incredible revelation. She laughed with a sigh of relief and voiced, "I've been waiting for you to get to this point of asking God what you want. Watch what God is

.

about to do for you. Watch what I say." We rejoiced and began to praise God for blessings to come. I realized that IF was a word I needed to relinquish.

It seemed life was taking a turn for the better. I traveled more for work as well as a few pleasure vacations. Things were becoming a little normal. I enjoyed getting out more. Weddings were no longer a dreaded chore. I had a better outlook on life as a whole. One Sunday morning, as my alarm clock blasted with my favorite gospel jam, I got up, dressed in my fine Sunday dress with shoes and hat to match, and headed out of the house for Sunday School. Our class consisted of several young people eager to learn more about the word of God. We enjoyed our teacher and what she presented every Sunday during our hour-long session. This particular Sunday, a young man joined our class that no one knew. Our teacher asked him to introduce himself to the class. He had a distinct accent that really caught my attention. He disclosed that he was from the Bahamas, graduated from college in the States with his bachelor's and master's degree, and was sent to St. Louis on a six-month job assignment. He stressed that he would only be here for six months. He appeared to be very studious and very knowledgeable of the word of God. He continued coming to Sunday School week after week and quickly was a Sunday morning regular. He became involved in our church and immediately started working with the young people, ministers, and the choir.

It was customary for us to go out as a group either after Sunday service or the weekly young people's service. With my antennas always on high alert, wondering if God was answering my prayer of sending my husband to my church, I pondered the idea maybe he was the one. I later found out he was engaged to be married to a young lady from his home country. I immediately shut down that inkling that he could be the one. Shortly after that, he missed a couple of Sundays. I was informed that he had gone back home to be married. Within a few weeks, he and his tall, brown-skinned beautiful wife came walking into Sunday School together. Our teacher congratulated them, along with everyone else in the class. I had no regrets; I stood by my belief that God would send my husband to my church.

About a month later, I noticed he continued to attend church and functioned in church as usual but did not see his wife. Curious but not bold enough to ask where she was, I assumed she had to finish up some things in the Bahamas and would be returning soon. To my surprise and probably many others, she never returned. We never saw her again. That's another book.

Several months later, I was at home after finishing a scrumptious meal of chicken wings, fries, and a salad. I decided this would be a night of total relaxation. I planned to watch my favorite Friday night tv lineup and enjoy some Swiss almond vanilla Häagen-Daz ice cream for dessert. My phone rang, and the caller ID registered a number I wasn't familiar with. Reluctantly I answered and heard the broad Caribbean accent of the young man from my church, "Good evening, how are you?" Startled, I responded, "Oh, fine, how are you?" I thought to myself, why is he calling me, and how did he get my number? After a few minutes of small talk, I didn't hesitate to ask, first and foremost, "So, where's your wife?" He explained, "Look, I'm not calling to hit on you or try to make a pass at you; I'm just looking for a friend." I thought to myself, yeah, right. To my amazement, he began to have what I called a normal, decent conversation. He asked me questions about my family and shared a lot about his. As the night went on, he shared his story about how his wife decided she didn't want to be married after two weeks, didn't want to live in the States, along with a host of other things she didn't want. He continued concluding, "She deeply hurt me." I could hear the devastation in his voice and wondered why he was telling me this. Not really knowing how to respond, I began to share scriptures of encouragement. That's just what we do! His openness made me feel comfortable sharing what I had been reluctant to share with anyone. After all, there was no motive or no romantic interest. What did I have to lose? To my disbelief, he had already known portions of my story. He was well-informed by someone at the church. What I thought would be a quick conversation turned into hours. I realized from that conversation that there was a level of trust; because we had shared so much of our personal lives, a genuine friendship was in the making. We continued to talk on a regular basis about life, issues, the Bible, and, of course, church.

Lesson learned: Patience

The Cambridge online dictionary defines patience as *the ability to wait or to continue doing something despite difficulties or to suffer without complaining or becoming annoyed.* Wow, that's a mouth full. Notice each task is separated by the word "or," but I would almost challenge

Cambridge and change the or to "and." There just isn't one definition for patience. We live in a culture where most of us want it now. Waiting isn't the norm, but in most situations, it is inevitable. We must wait. I found myself waiting often; the day of the week and what was going on around me determined my posture of waiting. Sometimes I was good and patient, "Ok, Lord, I know you hear me, and you'll come to see me," but most times, I was impatient, "Ok, Lord, where are you? Do you hear me?" Even in developing this friendship, God was teaching me to wait, not only to wait but wait with anticipation that He was in total control of this situation. We often quote that patience is a virtue, but do we really know what that means? First, let's define virtue. According to dictionary.com, virtue is defined as *moral excellence, goodness, and righteousness.* So, by putting both definitions together, patience is a virtue, to wait with an attitude of goodness and excellence. Not easy, I know, especially when faced with trials and tribulations. The Bible tells us in Romans 12:12, *"Rejoicing in hope; patient in tribulation, continuing instant in prayer."* How will you choose to wait, patiently or impatiently? Look back on a situation where you didn't wait patiently and make a choice to handle the next situation differently. It's up to you.

CHAPTER 10

Lord is This You?

And this is the confidence that we have in him, that, if we ask any thing according to his will, he heareth us. **- 1 John 5:14**

In all honesty, I enjoyed the time we talked, and at the end of each conversation, I looked forward to the next. Questions ran through my head. Am I developing feelings for him? Is he developing feelings for me? Hummmm. I quickly answered myself, no way! Two things about him made me tame my feelings. He was still married, in the process of a divorce, and was significantly younger than me. A few years younger was okay, but several years was almost a deal breaker for me. We continued our friendship which consisted of talking on the phone and seeing each other at church. It was a very difficult time for him dealing with the divorce, which was already in process but took almost two years to complete.

One evening while I was in my basement folding laundry and watching television, my phone rang. It was him. His voice sounded somewhat perplexed as he voiced, "Well, it's final." He was ready to put that portion of his life behind him but not ready to deal with the emotions that came along with it. As for us, there was a sense of freedom. Freedom to talk, freedom to hang out but to actually date? Not happening! We had developed a friendship, but moving forward into dating wasn't next on the agenda. Because of our past, we both had built Colosseum walls of protection around us that weren't easy to penetrate. We made a conscious decision not to allow anyone else to hurt us like we had been hurt before. We decided; friends we'll be.

I talked to my mentor and disclosed to her that I was torn. I told her, "I feel I have feelings for him, and it seems like he has feelings for me." She told me to pray about him, and she instructed me, "Ask God if this is the man he has for you, and ask if the actual answer to your prayer would be to send someone to your church." She told me, "Let go of all your deal breakers you have formed in your mind and let God do what He wants to do." In my mind, even if we moved forward in a relationship, I surely didn't want to be the R-word, a REBOUND. I began to seek God about this man. I was very specific in my prayers because I didn't want to make any mistakes.

On one Wednesday night, I attended Bible class as I usually did. I left work, grabbed a quick meal, and headed to church dressed in an off-white paisley print collarless blouse, and a brown plaid flared skirt. I knew he had an off-white collarless shirt. As lame as lame could be, I asked God, "If this is who you have for me, let him wear that shirt to church." When I got to church, I sat in my normal seat on the far-right side of the church while he sat in his usual seat on the far-left side. Trying hard to pay attention to the lesson, I glanced over and saw him in the very same shirt I had prayed about, and after service, when he approached me to speak, I saw his full attire. He had brown pants on. I could not believe my eyes. I was jaw-droppingly stunned that we were actually dressed alike. I tried to hide my expression as we walked out of church together. He asked, "Are you ok?" I giggled and replied, "Yes, I'm fine."

Even though we showed up in the same outfit, I never shared that with him, and I was still reluctant if he was for me. By this time, we were talking almost on a daily basis when he finally asked me out to a movie and dinner. I was excited, and Saturday evening could not come fast enough. When he came to my door, I ran to the mirror to make sure everything was in order. We exchanged small talk as we drove to the theatre. It appeared he was as nervous as I was. After the movie, we enjoyed a casual dinner at a local restaurant, where we sat and talked for hours. It appeared from the days following that we both were hesitant and perplexed as to where this relationship was going.

The next couple of months were like riding the roller coaster of our lives with no seat brace. Not realizing it then but knowing now: we were two hurt people trying to live a life of freedom from past hurts we still needed to deal with it. Those hurts interrupted and paralyzed a healthy future relationship between the two of us. I spent many evenings talking to my mentor, wetting her pillows, and telling her this wasn't worth it. Her encouragement remained the same, "You've got to trust God and let Him work on both of you, watch what I say."

We went from days of talking to each other to weeks where there was no conversation at all. Mentally I felt I couldn't deal with it. Still no commitment and no evidence of anything in the future. I decided, well, this is just not meant to be. My reason? He's too young. That was my answer to every roadblock we faced, and I was sticking to it. Later I talked to my mother about my ultimate dilemma of talking to someone younger than me. She voiced to me the notorious idiom, "Age is just a number." I thought thanks, Mom, not quite what I wanted to hear. Realizing I had feelings for him and was possibly falling in love but had no idea where our relationship was going, I decided to write him a letter. I wanted to make sure he received it, so I hand-delivered it to him while he was attending a meeting at a local bookstore. The long two-page letter could be summed up with let's just stop talking and seeing each other until we decide if there is a future for us. Tears of regret flooded my eyes for the next couple of days. I realized I had cut off any connection with him. Weeks passed, and I heard nothing from him. I would see him at church with no conversation. He would leave immediately after church, so there was no chance of running into him. I went back to God. My prayer was simple but to the point. Two requests: "First, God if (there I was using the word IF again), he's really for me make him call me soon, like within the next week or so, and second, let him be open with me and tell me exactly how he feels about me." I was extremely tired of riding this tumultuous journey and wanted to move on. Within a few days of my prayer, I got an unexpected call. Playing hard to get, I didn't answer the phone. I thought if he was really serious, he'd call back. Later that evening, feeling angry with myself for not answering the first call, after this was what I asked God for, I received the second call from him with an invitation to lunch. Ok, things were looking upward. Check; I asked God to let him call me after not hearing from him for so long. I accepted, and we met at one of our favorite Italian restaurants that weekend.

I dressed for the occasion in a nice red dress. Red is my favorite color, and whenever I wore red, I felt energized to accomplish whatever task was at hand. Not sure how that would play out in this situation, but why not! I arrived at the restaurant before him and was seated at the table alone. The restaurant covered its tables with a giant sheet of white paper and handed each guest crayons for writing on the paper. I sat and doodled as I waited for him to arrive, thinking he better not stand me up. Within minutes the hostess escorted him to the table. We ordered our food, and I waited patiently to hear what this meeting was about. While waiting for our food and during the meal, he talked about absolutely nothing. If I could have rolled my eyes without him seeing, I would have. We finished our meal, and the waitress handed him the bill. I'm sure total disappointment was written all over my face until the next couple of words came out of his mouth, "I realized a while back that I was falling in love with you but was afraid to actually say the words. I invited you here today to tell you I truly love you." That feeling of disappointment instantly changed to total disbelief that he actually said those words. I tried my best not to show my emotions. It was as if fireworks were sputtering out of my ears. However, I chose to keep a straight face. He picked up the crayons and started writing all the things he liked about me and what he thought of me. I was like, wow, this is so special. He continued by saying, "I believe we are too old to be dating like high schoolers, so I would really like for us to consider moving our friendship into a serious relationship with an intent for marriage. No, it wasn't a proposal, but it was a move in the right direction. With a shaky voice, I uttered, "I'll let you know." What just happened? I couldn't believe those words came from my own mouth. I had to think of something quick, so I said, "I need to talk to my pastor." He was actually fine with my answer because he knew the relationship I had with my pastor. We left the restaurant. Feeling overwhelmed, I immediately called my mentor and told her, "I'm on my way to your house with some exciting news that God has answered my prayers." When I arrived at her home, she asked, "What happened to you today? I can see a glow all over my face." I told her the whole story, and we both sat and cried, knowing God had answered our prayers.

I made an appointment with my pastor to discuss what I had experienced over the last 12 months. My pastor was very protective of me and asked as he looked at me with his eyes bucked, "Daughter, is this what you want?" As I dropped my chin to my chest, I quietly answered, "Yes, sir." He responded, "Well, I don't know too much about him, but I guarantee you I will." I really couldn't tell if he was happy for me or not, but he graciously gave me his blessings, and that was all I needed. Our meeting ended, and I left.

Being the thinker that I am, instead of rushing home to make "the call" with my decision to advance with the relationship, I waited a few days to process everything that had happened within the past few weeks. I rehashed the question from my pastor, "Daughter, is this what you want?" Do I really know this person? What about his family? So many questions rushed through my mind. Once again, I called my mentor. She explained, "You're experiencing fear." She reminded me, "This is what you prayed for," and told me, "You need to call him." The ball was in my court, and I decided to meet up with him to share the news. Despite all we both had been through, we both believed this was the will of God, and we were finally official!

Lesson learned: Hope

Dictionary.com defines Hope as *the feeling that what is wanted can be had or that events will turn out for the best.* The truth of the matter, I hoped this thing would work out. I felt I had invested too many feelings into something that possibly wasn't a part of my story or my future. The ESV version of Jeremiah 29:11 states, *"For I know the plans I have for you, declares the LORD, plans for welfare and not for evil, to give you a future and a hope."* After many hurdles, tears, and questions, God answered my prayers, and we were on the road to God's plans. Don't give up hope. It's a faith walk. It may not be evident or visible, but God's word is true. Hebrews 11:1 tells us, *"Now faith is the substance of things hoped for, the evidence of things not seen."*

CHAPTER 11

The Exchange

Now unto him that is able to do exceedingly abundantly above all that we ask or think, according to the power that worketh in us.
- Ephesians 3:20

This middle-aged woman who thought nobody would ever think of having a relationship with her was headed to the altar again. I asked him, "Did my past ever frighten you?" He confidently responded, "If God was in it, there was nothing to worry about." Wow! I was speechless. After I talked with him, we knew there were a few other people we needed to meet with. First and foremost, we met with our pastor, who gave us his blessings and chose a wedding date. He reminded my husband-to-be, "This is my daughter, and I will be keeping a close eye on you and this blooming relationship." We then met with my parents. It may have seemed old-fashioned considering our age, but he asked my father for permission to marry his daughter. I had already met his family after several crusade trips between our church and a local church in the Bahamas. Ironically until this very day, his mom confirms that she knew I was the one for him on our first meeting in the aisle of a local drug store close to her job. How she knew, only heaven knows, literally! We had about a year until our wedding date. We both wanted to get some things together before we were married. Once again, this brain of mine was racing on overload. Still questioning if I was making the right decision. We started pre-marital counseling and had about three sessions. For me, the counseling didn't address many questions that had me pondering. Marrying a man younger than me, from a different country, an Island man, and with a different cultural background stirred up my nerves a bit. At the time, I made more money than he, and I wondered how I would ever reach that dream of being able to stay at home one day. Oh well, as usual, I decided I'll deal with it when I must.

We were making plans; however, wait a minute, he hadn't officially proposed. We had looked at rings, and I picked a few that I liked, but nothing was on my left ring finger yet. Christmas was around the corner, and I thought for sure I would get it then. That didn't happen. My birthday was right after Christmas. Still no ring. I was getting a little flustered by now, but the next month was Valentine's Day. I knew it had to be my gift on this special day of love. As the day approached, he made plans to take me to dinner. I got dressed again in all red and waited for him to pick me up. We went to a fabulous restaurant and had a scrumptious steak dinner with all the trimmings. We enjoyed the evening, the conversation, and, of course, the meal. I waited, just knowing the next words out of his mouth would be, "Will you marry me?" After we finished eating, he politely asked, "Are you ready to go?" Not able to hide my facial expressions; dismay was written all over me. I quietly responded, "I guess so." I thought to myself, what a bummer!!!! As we started our drive to my home, or so I thought, there was dead silence in the car. So much so you could hear a pin drop. Then I noticed we weren't headed home. I rode in silence, wondering where we were going. The night was still young as we pulled up in front of a Jazz Venue that we both loved. As we entered the main lobby, he uttered to the attendant, "We have reservations." The ambiance was very romantic, with dimmed lights and candles lit on each table. We were escorted to our table and enjoyed the saxophonist that played an array of jazz love songs throughout the evening. We ordered dessert, talked, laughed, and enjoyed the music. While waiting for the dessert to come, in the middle of our conversation, he said, "I want to officially ask you to marry me." What I had hoped and waited for had finally happened, and with the excitement, I couldn't find words. From the inside pocket of his suit jacket, he pulled out the ring. A tear rolled down my face, and I said yes as he placed the ring on my finger. People around us began to clap and congratulate us. I actually lost track of everything; I sat and stared at my ring finger for the rest of the evening. I was literally on cloud nine. I couldn't wait until the next day to make my rounds to family' and friends' homes to show off my ring. We were really official now! The planning seemed more realistic now.

We decided we would buy a home together. That began our search for the perfect house. I assured him, "When I walk into the house, I will know if it is the one." His patience was running out with me as we toured house after house. I would say, "Sorry, this just isn't it," until one day, we walked into a house where I had that feeling: this is the one. The house sat on a cul-de-sac in what seemed to be a quiet neighborhood. It was a five-bedroom house with a fully finished basement and an attraction in the basement bathroom, a definite winner, a large hot tub. I could tell he wasn't impressed when we first walked in because the hallway and family room walls were painted baby pink. I looked at him and the real estate agent and said, "This is it!" The look on his face was, "REALLY?" and he gasped, "Pink walls," but I pointed out, "We can always paint." We purchased that home, and he moved into it a month before our wedding. It seemed the time had flown by, and I was walking down the aisle within a matter of time.

Of course, everyone thinks their wedding is the best, but I knew for sure ours was. The sanctuary was adorned with beautiful tall white columns at the altar, filled with abundant greenery, and two floral arches in the aisle. The theme of the day was "The Red Rose." As I was escorted down the aisle to the tune of "To God be the Glory," tears streamed down my beautifully made-up face. I knew God had done something really special for me to let me see the day I thought would never happen again. Everything was breathtaking. We later gathered that afternoon with about 200 guests at our reception, which was filled with so many surprises for me. He wanted Caribbean Calypso music, and I wanted a Jazz saxophonist, so we had both. To my amazement, he had added decorations I wasn't aware of and a local Jazz soloist to perform an array of selections dedicated especially to me. We retired to the hotel room to enjoy each other and prepare for an early morning flight on Sunday.

Another surprise, I didn't know where we were going on our honeymoon. Our first flight was to Chicago. Still oblivious to our final destination, I asked, "Can you tell me now?" He never responded, only smiled as we walked toward the gate of our second flight. I read on the illuminated sign, Rome, Italy. The emotions of shock and excitement clashed together as I stood in a fixed gaze. He was smiling from ear to ear, knowing he had pulled off the surprise of the century. I couldn't believe it! Our layover was a little over an hour, but I refused to leave the gate, not taking a chance of missing this flight. Finally, it was time to board, and we gathered our belongings to load the plane. The long 10-hour flight didn't seem as long because we flew through the night, and the anticipation flushed the feelings of dreading the long flight. We arrived in Rome, Italy, the next morning and checked into our hotel, where we would stay the night and then travel on a bus tour for the next 11 days throughout Italy. We adored the sites of hundred years old buildings, huge ornate chapels, The Vatican, The Colosseum, monuments, secluded islands, beaches, and so much more. The delicious meals were different from what we had experienced in our different cultures but were absolutely mouthwatering. It was a wonderful trip I will never forget. We returned to our new home, new life, and new beginnings. Was this man part of my double blessing? Absolutely.

After about three years of marriage, the subject of children came up, not a subject discussed in pre-marital counseling, so he didn't know my thoughts, and I really didn't know his. Thinking back on my days of volunteering at the children's home, all things were in order for a possible adoption. I was married now. I never entertained the thought of adopting as a single mom. I was ready to sign up for the adoption classes. One problem, though: he was not on board with it. I thought, "You've got to be kidding me. Where did this come from, God?" Yes, I questioned God. I just figured everything would fall into place once we got married. Not at all. His response to the idea of adopting was, "I'm not very familiar with the adoption process." He wanted biological children. What? Houston, we got a problem. Remember, I'm older, significantly older than him. In my mind, biological possibilities were shut down years ago. Nothing I said could convince him to even consider adoption. At this point, I had no other choice but to pray about it. I wrote in my journal, "Lord, you gotta talk to this man; I'm serious!" I left it alone and asked my mentor to pray about it with me. She assured me by quoting Proverbs 21:1, *"The king's heart is in the hand of the LORD, as the rivers of water: he turneth it whithersoever he will."* "Allow God to deal with your husband, watch what I say." After a few months, out of the blue, he said to me on a Friday evening, "Hey, do you think we can get into a class for adoption?" I couldn't believe what I was hearing. I asked, "What did you say?" He repeated himself. I said, "I'll call my sister-in-law and see if she can get us in a class." When I called her, I was sure she could hear the excitement in my voice. I was screaming from the top of my lungs, "He changed his mind, he changed his mind. Can you please get us into a class as soon as possible before he changes back?" She pulled some strings and was able to sign us up for a class that began the following Tuesday. The classes were very informative and lasted several weeks, but the whole process was long and tedious. So many papers to fill out, questions, interviews, and home visits. It was as if the FBI was investigating us for a possible crime. We had to prepare a home study that outlined everything about us. This home study would be used by a group of advocates for a child to determine if we were a good fit. Finally, we passed everything with flying colors and were approved to become adoptive parents to our request for two babies or toddler kids. Our prayer together was, "Lord, you know the child you have for us and where they are. Bring our family together." The process of approval was nerve-racking, and at the beginning, a whole new set of worries surfaced. How do you do motherhood successfully? Is there a manual? A book I can read? I was so terrified and didn't even have a kid in my home yet. I shared my feelings with my mentor, mother, sister, and, of course, my sister-in-law and always got the answer, "Oh, you'll be fine." Somehow that didn't suffice at all. I handled my nerves to the best of my ability as we waited patiently for a child. The process involved our case manager sending us a photo of a child, and if we were interested, our home study was submitted, and we'd wait eagerly to see if we were chosen. To our dismay, this happened four times, and each time we were not chosen. My husband was becoming very frustrated. I mean to the point of giving up. I reminded him of our prayer and assured him God had a child for us. We had to believe that.

My husband regularly traveled out of town for work, and on this particular day, he had gone out of town. I received a call one winter Wednesday afternoon from the agency we were working with. The social worker explained, "I have a little 19-month-old boy that I need a decision on by tomorrow to be placed on Friday." She told me, "I don't have a picture or a profile on him, but looking for a placement, and I do believe he would be a great fit for you and your husband." I couldn't believe this was really about to go down. I called my husband and rehashed the conversation to the best of my ability and told him that we needed to make a decision by the next day. He immediately said, "Yes, of course." I recapped, "Did you hear me say, no picture, no profile?" He assured me, "Yes, I heard you. I'm ok with that." I thought oh my, this is really happening. Talk about scared with capital S C A R E D. I called the social worker back and said, "Yes, we are interested. What's the next step?" She advised, "You won't have to go through the presentation of our home study or the long process of decision-making by the group of advocates for him. Just meet me at my office on Friday at 1:00 pm." We shared the news with our family members and requested prayer for us. We both took the day off from work and drove silently, nervously, to pick up our potential son. We arrived about 15 minutes before 1 pm and sat nervously in the car. We walked into the building, holding hands, knowing this meeting would change our lives forever. I was literally shaking in my boots. We were escorted into the case worker's office and sat silently, waiting for her to wake him up from a nap and bring him to us. When we saw him immediately, all nerves and anxiety miraculously left. We were so excited. We praised God for orchestrating our process and finalized the adoption in four months instead of the normal six months.

Our son adjusting to us and us adjusting to him wasn't as easy as we thought. He accepted my husband more readily than me, but we worked through it with many tears and prayers. It took several months for him to adjust to our daily routine of daycare, dinner time, playtime, and bedtime and weekends of exploring child adventures and church. Unexpectantly about a year and a half later, we received another call from another agency. We did want two kids, but at this time, we weren't seeking to adopt again so soon, but what the lady said on the other end left us with no choice. She said, "I am a social worker, and I believe you have the brother of a baby boy I am trying to place." She continued, "I petitioned the courts to open your file, something they normally don't do to get your phone number. I was wondering, are you interested in adopting him?" I couldn't believe what I was hearing. We didn't hesitate and agreed that we would start the process of adopting him. The boys had several visits together and bonded immediately. God had done it again. Shortly after we moved him into our home, the adoption process was final, and our family was complete. Two boys, two years apart, and biological brothers. Who could ask for anything any better than this? Were they a part of my double blessing? Without a doubt, both of them!

Prior to us getting the boys, my husband experienced some changes in his job that affected our finances. He was called into the office one day and told he would be moved to another division and that his current salary would be reduced by $15,000. This made a significant impact on our current lifestyle. He was full of rage and, of course, immediately started searching for another job while remaining at his current job. We managed to put things in order and curtail our spending to make it work. He submitted application after application with no hope in sight. After months of searching and many disappointments, he was interviewed several times by one company and felt very hopeful. Within a few weeks, an offer letter was in our mailbox, and we both were so excited. Before he could call with a formal acceptance, the company informed him that they would not be able to move forward with the offer due to some undisclosed problem. I was saddened, but not as much as he was. It was as if someone had snatched the wind out of his lungs. After a few days of moping around, he started the search again. We prayed and believed God that something would come through. About three months later, he received a call from the same company that had sent him the offer letter. They explained that they had some internal issues but were now ready to make him the offer if he was still interested. He accepted the offer and started working for a company where there was great potential for growth.

Later, another unexpected cut in salary occurred; I was laid off from my job. I started doing contract work to try and supplement my salary; however, my desire was to be a stay-at-home mom. I continued to work, but at least I wasn't traveling anymore. For the next three and half years, I managed to work, come home and do the normal routine of a working mom, still waiting for the day to kiss that lifestyle goodbye. Our plan to pay off as many bills as possible worked well. By now, it was time for my oldest son to start kindergarten. My husband and I both decided it was time for me to come home. Finally, my dream of becoming a stay-at-home mom became a reality. No words could express my feelings. Yes, it took sacrifices, but it was wholeheartedly worth it. I devoted 100% of my time to taking care of my family. In the next couple of years, I was available for field trips and volunteering at the school. I met a lot of moms that had been doing this stay-at-home life all their married life. The boys were in a private school which didn't seem to be a good match for them. By the time my oldest son completed second grade, after much thought, we decided to pull both boys out of school and homeschool them. It wasn't the easiest journey, but I would not trade it for the time and bonding of my boys. I sacrificed a lot and said no to many things, but I was assured that this was the plan that God had specifically for me. About that salary issue that I kind of struggled with, when we first got married, my husband worked his way up in his new company, and his salary skyrocketed about five times more than mine. Yes, I said five. Yes, God did it! Was this "by faith" move a part of my double blessing? Absolutely!

God has blessed me with more than I could have ever imagined. If I started naming all the blessings God has bestowed on me, I would have to write another book. The blessings are the amenities of my double. My double is my husband and my children. This journey that started almost 30 years ago has allowed me to see the miraculous power of God working in my life. It was almost 10 years from the day my first husband died that the Lord blessed me with my current husband of almost 20 years (double). To go from the **SHAME** of wondering if anyone would ever want me again, if anyone would love me again, if anyone would desire a woman whose husband died of AIDS, to God sending me a man all the way from the Bahamas to my church to love me as Christ loved the church is mind-blowing. He is a God-loving, God-fearing man that loves me and will do anything for me. There isn't anything that I desire that he isn't going to try and get for me. He treats me like a queen. Do we have a perfect marriage? Absolutely not! We have gone through some of the same things that most couples go through, but we are determined to go through this thing called life together with God with us.

The second part of my double is that I have two boys who call me mom. Being a mom is said to be the most important and hardest job a woman can have. Even though I did not have any biological children, God blessed me to mother two amazing boys. At the time of writing this book, I am raising two teenagers. Enough said. I say that to say everything isn't perfect. We've made mistakes and had challenges, but we thank God that He chose us to parent our boys. God fulfilled in my life: for your **SHAME,** I will give you double (my husband and my boys).

Lesson learned: Promises

The Cambridge online dictionary defines promise as *telling someone that you will certainly do something.* From the day that my mentor quoted Isaiah 61:7, *"For your shame ye shall have double; and for confusion they shall rejoice in their portion: therefore in their land they shall possess the double: everlasting joy shall be unto them,"* I had no idea what the fulfillment of that scripture was in my life. All I could do was stand on His promises. He said it, and even though it took years, He blessed me with double: my husband and my boys. The Sunday after my first husband's funeral, I walked into that church covered in **SHAME**, BUT GOD! I can truly say I thank God for my double. Whatever promise He has made to you, believe it. His word says, *"The Lord is not slack concerning his promise, as some men count slackness' but is longsuffering to us-ward, not willing that any should perish but that* *all should come to repentance."* 2 Peter 3:9. Stand on his promises in whatever situation you are facing. He's so faithful.

CHAPTER 12

No more SHAME

Behold, at that time I will undo all that afflict thee: and I will save her that halteth, and gather her that was driven out; and I will get them praise and fame in every land where they have been put to shame. **- Zephaniah 3:19**

There's a familiar saying, "Hindsight is 20/20," and often so true. As I look back over my life, I see so much. First and foremost, God had me all the time. He precisely and flawlessly orchestrated every season of my life. Each lesson learned has allowed me to realize just how much He loves me and cares for me. He gave me **Confidence** in those times when I was swayed to doubt the next step. He was my **Refuge** anytime I faced trouble or anxiety. He gave me the **Endurance** I needed to hold on and not give up. He increased my **Faith** to believe everything would be all right despite what it looked like. When He spoke, He gave me the **Assurance** that His word would come to pass. When I was unaware of the dangers attacking me, He was my **Protection.** He reminded me how He forgave me, and the **Forgiveness** of others was not optional but essential. He taught me to practice **Contentment** instead of complaining. Many times, He would whisper to me, "**Patience,** my daughter," when it felt like I was depleted of the ability to wait. He gave me **Hope** that there was a rainbow on the horizon after the many storms. Dreams do come true, and He fulfills every one of His **Promises.** Lastly, He graciously showed me that **Miracles** still happen, and because I'm an heir of my Father, I'm also entitled to them. I can say things would have been much easier had I realized a lot of these lessons years ago. I see them as stepping stones that brought me to the place where I am now, **UNASHAMED**. SHAME ON ME—NO MORE! I will not go back to that place. Those masks have been taken off and will not be adorned anymore.

As I stated before, God blessed me with double, and I can't thank Him enough for what He has done for me. I'm so grateful, but I believe the greatest lesson, and what I can help others with, is being free from the bondage of **SHAME**. I didn't realize how **SHAME** had captured and shackled me in chains; I could not break away from it. **SHAME** is something the enemy uses to strip us of our identity. He uses deception to whisper in our ears things that are not true. This isn't something new for him; he began way back during the fall. The book of Genesis chapter 2, verse 25, states, *"And they were both naked, the man and his wife, and were not ashamed."* After the fall in chapter 3, Adam and Eve realized they were naked and hid. *"And the Lord God called unto Adam, and said unto him. Where art thou? And he said, I heard thy voice in the garden, and I was afraid, because I was naked; and I hid myself,"* Genesis 3:9-10. When the serpent spoke to Eve, he messed with her identity. You see, according to Genesis 1:27, Adam and Eve were created in the image of God. He told her that when she ate the fruit, she would be like God. Hello! They were already like God, created in His image. He deceived her by telling her she could be something she already was. He distorted her identity. God asked Adam, "Who told you you were naked?" Has the enemy tricked you into thinking you're something or someone that you're not? Who told you you are a disgrace? Who told you you are worthless? Who told you you are a nobody? Who told you you are a failure? Who told you you should be ashamed of yourself? The enemy. Psalm 139:13-14 states, *"For you created my inmost being; you knit me together in my mother's womb. I praise you because I am fearfully and wonderfully made; your works are wonderful, I know that full well."* What is He saying? What He created, as a matter of fact, anything He creates, is beautiful, flawless, wonderful, and extraordinary, including you. Mufasa in The Lion King told Simba, "You have forgotten who you are. Remember, you belong to the king." Remember who you are. We are sons and daughters of the Almighty King of Kings and Lord of Lords. Remember who you are.

As He knitted us together, He equipped us for whatever was coming in our lives. He prepared us to handle the most difficult situations we would face. When a seamstress knits together a piece of apparel, it's very unlikely that they can duplicate that item exactly. One stitch may cause a difference in the outcome of the garment. Our Father took the time to prepare us for our outcome in life. Yours is different from mine, but He did not create us to fail. He didn't create us to lose the identity that He formed in us. We are His children made in His image. Do not let the enemy steal that from you. **SHAME** tried to steal what God knitted in me in my mother's womb. But thank God for the victory. I am no longer suffering and bound by the chains of **SHAME**; you don't have to be either. I am thankful for my double but more so grateful that I can declare, **SHAME ON ME—NO MORE**! No more will I hide behind the guilt of my past.

If you are suffering from situations in your past that have you thinking you're not worth it, get help. Seek counsel from someone who can be a help to you. I did not have a counselor, but I am so grateful for the mentor God placed in my life, who walked side by side with me, cried with me, prayed with and for me, and was instrumental in helping me. Don't walk your journey alone; reach out to a pastor, a friend, or a professional counselor. You are not alone!

CHAPTER 13

A Miraculous Curveball

*The thief cometh not, but for to steal, and to kill, and to destroy:
I am come that they might have life, and that they might have it
more abundantly. - **John 10:10***

During writing this book, I was thrown a curve ball I totally did not expect. I did not see it coming and questioned why it had to happen to me and why at this time in my life. I became afflicted in my body, and even though well beyond the age of menopause, I started bleeding. Because it was something, I had dealt with five years ago, I thought nothing of it. I had polyps removed from my uterus; they were all benign at that time. I made an appointment with my doctor, and knowing my history, she explained my polyps had returned and scheduled me for a procedure to have them removed again. I went through the procedure and went back to meet with her a week later. To my surprise and disbelief, she explained, "You had one large polyp, and it was grade 1 endometrium cancer." I could not believe what my ears were hearing. Holding back the tears, I listened as she explained, "I removed the entire polyp, and providing the cancer did not spread, a total abdominal hysterectomy would solve the problem." I was completely numb. No one wants to hear the words you and cancer in the same sentence. I went home, talked to my husband, and said, "Well, dear, this was not what I wanted to hear." For the next couple of days, I wrestled in my mind, what next? I was devastated. But as the days went by, I began to talk to the Lord and the enemy. I realized this book is being written to encourage so many women, and the devil does not want it published. I began to see the attack of the enemy, and I spoke into the atmosphere, "Satan, you will not stop this publication." I had just finished writing about my past, started writing the chapter on forgiveness, and next, I was to start on the double blessings.

I was referred to another doctor. My husband and I went to see her to talk about the hysterectomy. She explained just as my doctor, "Hopefully, the cancer is contained in the polyp and uterus, and everything will be fine. I will remove everything, including several lymph nodes, and have it all tested by the pathologist." Anytime the words lymph nodes and cancer are mentioned together, it's a feeling that's difficult to even put a word to. My husband and I walked out of her office feeling confident the cancer had not spread. That's what we stood on. I didn't share the diagnosis with many people, only a few that I was sure would stand in agreement with me for a miracle. I didn't want anyone worrying about me or feeling sorry for me. No negative thinking was allowed. This was not the order of the day! My surgery was scheduled about 8 weeks after my initial appointment.

During this time, many thoughts raced through my head. A lot of what-ifs! However, I chose to stand on the promises of God. In the meantime, I was invited to a woman's conference, ironically, by my publicist, and believe it or not, the conference was entitled "I Survived." At first, I declined the invitation thinking I would be out of town on the dates of the conference, only to realize I had the dates wrong. I informed her I would be able to attend and had been given VIP seating which meant I was able to sit in the front section of the sanctuary. As I entered the conference, I chose my seat in the center on about the fourth row. Praise and worship began, and immediately following, the Praise Dancers assembled on the stage. Three women, one in the lead position and the other two in the background adorned in beautiful royal blue garments, began to give God praise through their hands and feet motions, gracefully flowing to the beat of the music. The swaying was simply an awesome act of giving God the reverence He was due. They finished the first song and began a second song. During this dance, two other ladies joined them on the floor with a banner that each held and waved in a motion that seemed like they were creating an altar of worship. The lead sister came down from the stage and began to dance alone on the floor. She appeared to scope the audience as if she was searching for someone. She approached a young lady and ushered her under the banner that the two young ladies were waving. She returned to the center aisle and once again began to peruse the audience. She started in my direction. In all honesty, my thoughts were, oh no, not me! As she got closer, she extended her hand to me, and what seemed as if a Thrush grabbed me, escorted me to the banner altar, and released me. I immediately fell to the floor and felt like I was kneeling before the Almighty God. Tears began to run down my face, and I felt the presence of God overshadow me as if He was rocking me in His arms. Suddenly I heard the voice of a young lady singing, and it appeared she was writing a song as she was standing there singing. All I heard was her continuing to say, "A miraculous healing." Tears rushed down my face even more. I felt God was speaking directly to me. Even though I was only there for a few minutes, it felt like I had been in God's presence for hours. I gathered myself, arose from the floor, and returned to my seat. As the service went on, the speaker was introduced, and she took the podium and read her scripture for the evening message. She read the story of Hannah, and her sermon topic was, "I'm expecting a miracle." As I sat in awe hearing the word miracle again, I felt God had created this conference for me and me alone. She emphasized that there were uncommon healings and uncommon miracles in the room that evening. She went on to say some ladies in this place tonight have experienced some difficult times, and some things have caused us great **SHAME**. Literally, I felt as if the butterflies in my stomach were fighting World War I, as I thought, where is she going with this? She then quoted a portion of Isaiah 61:7, *"For your shame ye shall have double…"* I almost fell off my seat. I texted my publicist and asked why this lady was all in my book. It was God's way of letting me know in the midst of this curveball, He was right there with me and to keep writing. I've got a story to tell. I left that service driving home feeling the very presence of God riding in my car with me. Oh, what a blessing to attend that conference.

Each night from the day we received the diagnosis, the Lord instructed me to have my husband anoint me with oil and pray over me. On the day of the surgery, we prayed again and believed God for a miracle. I went into surgery believing in God. Everyone in the hospital was so positive. That really helped me because I made it my business not to entertain any negative thoughts or receive any negative energy. The surgery went well, and I was sent home to recuperate.

A week after the surgery, I received a call from the doctor. She asked me, "How is your pain level? Have you had any complications?" I answered, "The pain is getting better, and so far, no complications." She stated, "I was very pleased with the surgery, and I sent everything to the pathologist for testing. I have good news. The cancer did not spread. NO CANCER! No further treatment necessary." I believed in God, and it came to pass. I praise Him for yet another miracle He performed in my life. I could hear the Lord saying to me, "Daughter, thy faith has made thee whole." By the way, I wrote this chapter in faith, believing that the doctor would call me back to say, I have good news, and that's exactly what she said. It was written six weeks before my surgery, and I am yet rejoicing for the miraculous curveball that He sent my way. Look what God did!

Lesson learned: Miracles

According to dictionary.com, the word miracle is defined in several ways, but the one I will focus on is *such an effect or event manifesting or considered as a work of God*. Some don't believe that miracles still exist. They see it as something that took place in the Bible, not something possible in our day. In essence, we are all walking miracles. Every day we can attribute our very being to a miracle of God. I prayed for a miracle, and I believed God. He did it. Matthew 19:26, Mark 10:27, and Luke 18:27 speak of that with man, it is impossible, but with God, all things are possible.

> *But Jesus beheld them, and said unto them, With men this is impossible; but with God all things are possible. - Matthew 19:26*
> *And Jesus looking upon them saith, With men it is impossible, but not with God: for with God all things are possible. - Mark 10:27*
> *And he said, The things which are impossible with men are possible with God. - **Luke 18:27***

Miracles! Trust God for whatever miracle you need in your life.

Bibliography

Chapter 1

"Confidence." Merriam-Webster.com. Merriam-Webster, 2023. Web. 13 March 2023.

Chapter 2

"Refuge." Dictionary.com. 2023. 13 March 2023.

Chapter 3

The American Cancer Society medical and editorial content team. "What Is Kaposi Sarcoma?" *American Cancer Society*, 19 April 2018, Cancer.org.

"Endurance." Merriam-Webster.com. Merriam-Webster, 2023. Web. 13 March 2023.

Chapter 4

"Faith." Merriam-Webster.com. Merriam-Webster, 2023. Web. 13 March 2023.

Chapter 5

"Assured." Merriam-Webster.com. Merriam-Webster, 2023. Web. 13 March 2023.

Chapter 6

"Update: Mortality Attributable to HIV Infection Among Persons Aged 25-44 Years—United States, 1991 and 1992." Center for Disease Control-MMWR Weekly, 19 November 1993, cdc.gov.

"Protect." Dictionary.com. 2023. 13 March 2023.

Chapter 7

"Forgive." kingjamesbibledictionary.com. King James Bible Dictionary. 2023. Web. 13 March 2023.

Chapter 8

Jakes, T.D. Lyrics to "I'm Your First Husband." Performed by Soloist Bettye Ransom Nelson. Integrity Music, 1996. Pandora.com, https://www.pandora.com/artist/td-jakes/woman-thou-art-loosed/im-your-1st-husband/TR3PfjdjfmXx33J.

"Contented." Merriam-Webster.com. Merriam-Webster, 2023. Web. 13 March 2023.

Chapter 9

"Patience." Dictionary.cambridge.org. Cambridge Dictionary, 2023 Web. 13 March 2023.

"Virtue." Dictionary.com. 2023. 13 March 2023.

Chapter 10

"Hope." Dictionary.com. 2023. 13 March 2023.

Chapter 11

"Promise." Dictionary.cambridge.org. Cambridge Dictionary, 2023 Web. 13 March 2023.

Chapter 13

"Miracle." Dictionary.com. 2023. 13 March 2023.